THE
MEANING
OF
MALLARMÉ

BY THE SAME AUTHOR

Etudes sur Rimbaud, Paris, Nizet, 1959
Mallarmé, sa pensée dans sa poésie, Paris, Corti, 1962
Symbolism, London, Methuen, 1971
Verlaine, The Athlone Press, London, 1973
Rimbaud, The Athlone Press, London, 1979

ACKNOWLEDGEMENTS

Thanks are due to The Carnegie Trust for the Universities of Scotland and to The University of Aberdeen for their generous help with the publication of this volume.

THE
MEANING
OF
MALLARMÉ

A bilingual edition of his

POÉSIES

and

UN COUP DE DÉS

translated and introduced

by

CHARLES CHADWICK

SCOTTISH CULTURAL PRESS

First published 1996
Scottish Cultural Press
PO Box 106
Aberdeen AB11 7ZE
Tel: 01224 583777
Fax: 01224 575337

British Library Cataloguing in Publication Data
A catalogue record for this book is available
from the British Library

ISBN: 1 898218 29 3

Printed and bound in Great Britain by
Cromwell Press, Melksham, Wiltshire

CONTENTS

PREFACE

'Mallarmé', one of his contemporaries is reputed to have said, 'is untranslatable – even into French'. There is no denying the truth of this caustic comment if the would-be translator tries to keep too close to the original text. Mallarmé's poetry is usually so condensed, its syntax frequently so tortuous and its meaning sometimes so concealed that, as it stands, it is indeed often untranslatable. It is for this reason that, in the following pages, the original text has, on occasions, been expanded in the translation and obscure images have been interpreted in order to achieve the goal of giving meaning to the poems. Whether this meaning is always Mallarmé's own is, of course, a moot point, but most of the high priests of the Mallarmé cult would probably agree that the exegeses adopted in the translations are broadly correct, although they would no less probably disagree with the translator, and with one another, on numerous points of detail, some of which are indicated in the notes at the end of this volume. Similarly, although there are different views with regard to certain aspects of Mallarmé's thought, it is unlikely that anyone would quarrel with the broad outline of the development of his ideas given in the introduction. Purists may, however, disapprove of the consequent re-arrangement, in chronological order according to the dates when they were begun, of the poems Mallarmé included in his edition of his *Poésies*, even though there is no apparent significance in the order in which the poems are set out in that edition. They may also disapprove of the way in which the poems are grouped under what it is hoped are useful headings, the omission of a small number of poems tangential to the main thrust of Mallarmé's ideas, the inclusion of three sonnets which were omitted from the *Poésies* but which are more relevant to those ideas, and the addition of the immensely difficult but vitally important *Un Coup de Dés*.

to N O'B

INTRODUCTION

AN OUTLINE OF MALLARMÉ'S LIFE AND WORK

Mallarmé, like Baudelaire a generation earlier, was obsessed with the longing to turn his back on the harsh world of reality and to seek refuge in an ideal world. This may have been an attitude inherited from Romanticism, but in Baudelaire's case it has also been suggested that it was due in no small measure to personal factors, namely the double blow of his father's death when he was six years old and his mother's second marriage eighteen months later. Mallarmé's childhood was somewhat similar in that his mother died in 1847 when he was five years old and his father remarried fifteen months later, but a third blow was to fall with the death of his sister Maria in 1857. It is scarcely surprising therefore that, with a greater urgency even than Baudelaire, Mallarmé should have wanted to escape from a world that had treated him so cruelly. It is interesting to note that in one of his earliest poems, 'Apparition', written in 1862 when he was twenty, the girl Mallarmé is on his way to meet, and who is no doubt his future wife Maria Gerhard, is metamorphosed in the final lines into an ethereal figure, part mother, part sister. But although he thus seems to be reaching out through this world towards another world, he also expresses, in the central lines of the poem, the almost contrary view that an ideal can never be transformed into reality since it thereby loses its ideal quality. He goes even further than this in 'Les Fenêtres', written a year later, and in a brief and oddly bitter reference to 'une peau virginale et de jadis' he seems to be implying that the gap between the ideal and the reality has widened and that the transformation of the one into the other has left not merely the slight 'parfum de tristesse' of 'Apparition', but the deeper feeling of regret and disappointment that he had specifically denied in the earlier poem. So although Mallarmé married Maria Gerhard in August 1863, three or four months after writing 'Les Fenêtres', and although their marriage was a lasting and, to all outward appearances, a tolerably happy one, it seems clear that this first attempt to find in love a successful refuge from the world was a short-lived one. His vain hope of thus transforming his ideal into reality is indeed already replaced in 'Les Fenêtres' by an outright rejection of the latter and an overwhelming desire to flee towards the former. This could well be explained by yet another blow that Mallarmé had suffered, for less than a month after his twenty-first birthday and just before he wrote 'Les Fenêtres' his father had died in April 1863. It may possibly be for this reason that, in contrasting the pain and ugliness of the real world with the beauty and happiness of the ideal world, Mallarmé uses, in the first half of the poem, the allegory of a dying man turning his back on the sick room and longing for a new life in the sky beyond the windows. In the second half of the poem however, where the allegory is interpreted, the nature of the ideal world is left vague and ill-defined, as is the method of attaining it. Art or mystical experience are two ways of reaching his shadowy Eldorado that Mallarmé mentions in the curiously casual thirteenth line of the poem, but in the final lines he fears that he does not possess these artistic or mystical powers, or at least that such powers as he may possess in his 'ailes sans plumes' are inadequate for the task of soaring up towards the ideal world.

This feeling of inadequacy rapidly became increasingly acute, so much so that in 'L'Azur', written in January 1864, there is a complete reversal of the theme of 'Le Fenêtres'. Mallarmé now turns his back on the unattainable ideal world and instead of pouring scorn on ordinary mortals 'wallowing in happiness' as he had put it, he now wants, on the contrary, to belong to this 'bétail heureux des hommes'. The reason for this *volte face* is that whereas Mallarmé had at first merely longed for the ideal world in a vague kind of way and had done no more than suggest that art might be one way of attaining it, in the six months separating 'Les Fenêtres' from 'L'Azur' he had tried to define his ideas more clearly and had failed. He had discovered that to write something other than mere descriptive verse dealing with objects in the real world, to try and give poetic form to an immaterial world was an apparently impossible task. Yet it was one which he could not escape, as the last two verses of 'L'Azur' make clear, for although the preceding verses describe Mallarmé's failure to write poetry evocative of the ideal world, they lead up to an account of his failure to shake off his obsession with that world.

In fact, however, Mallarmé did manage to free himself from his obsession in his next two poems, 'Las de l'amer repos' and 'Les Fleurs', where, reluctant to lapse into complete idleness and yet tired of vainly struggling to evoke an ideal world in his poetry, he chooses a middle course and consoles himself with writing facile, descriptive verse about the world around him with its flowers, its lakes and its crescent moons. But his escape was to be a very temporary one, for in 'Le Pitre châtié', written initially in March 1864 although extensively re-written much later, Mallarmé is chastised precisely because he has been a traitor to his true vocation, that of the meditative, intellectual kind of poet, choosing his words as carefully as an actor chooses his gestures. In 'Soupir' therefore the wheel comes full circle and Mallarmé is back again in something of the same state of mind he had been in at the end of 'L'Azur', except that he is now reconciled to his fate and sadly recognises that, however long and difficult his task may be, he has no alternative but to try and define his ideal world and to find means of evoking it in his poetry.

If 'Soupir' echoes to some extent 'L'Azur', so too does one of the most celebrated and compelling of Mallarmé's poems, the sonnet beginning 'Le vierge, le vivace et le bel aujourd'hui' which, although published only in 1884, undoubtedly dates from some twenty years before. Its theme is clearly that of someone haunted by an ambition he is powerless to achieve. As each day dawns he is full of hope that he will at last manage to launch himself towards his goal, but he repeatedly finds not only that he is unable to do so but that the more he hesitates and reflects and ponders the more he succumbs to a fatal inactivity. Inspiration, of the kind he wants, has deserted Mallarmé, and yet he refuses now to yield, as he had done in 'Las de l'amer repos' and 'Les Fleurs', to the temptation of writing verse of an easier kind. Instead he turns to poetry dealing indirectly and allegorically with his own problem in two of his best-known works, 'Hérodiade' and 'L'Après-midi d'un faune'. Both of these dramatic poems underwent many changes and modifications over the years and 'Hérodiade' was in fact never completed, but there is little doubt that the scene between Hérodiade and her nurse, which was the only part ever published by Mallarmé himself, dates from 1864-1865 and that 'L'Après-midi d'un faune', as far as its essential features are concerned, dates from 1865-1866.

The heroine of 'Hérodiade' is the Biblical character more generally known as Salome, but Mallarmé preferred the alternative name so as to emphasise that he was concerned not with the sensuous dancer of popular legend but, on the contrary, with an ascetic figure who is repelled by the slightest contact with the sensual world and who, in the later, uncompleted stages of the play, was to demand the head of John the Baptist because he had inadvertently caught a glimpse of her naked body. An obvious explanation of this curious reversal of the character generally attributed to Salome is that Mallarmé is using her as a symbol of his own situation. He himself implied this when he later said of the poem: 'Je m'y étais mis tout entier sans le savoir', and Hérodiade's rejection of the easy pleasures of the senses with which the nurse repeatedly tempts her clearly continues the theme of the immediately preceding poems in which Mallarmé had persistently turned his back on the superficialities of the real world. There is, however, a change of tone, for the period of failure, despair and resignation is over. It is true that complete success has not yet been achieved, but Mallarmé is at least convinced, judging by Hérodiade's firmness of purpose and the expectant note on which the scene ends, that he is now on the verge of defining the nature of his ideal world.

Although 'L'Après-midi d'un faune' was written as a relaxation after 'Hérodiade' and although Mallarmé never actually said that into this poem too he had put all his thoughts and feelings without realising it, it could nevertheless be argued that this is in fact the case. One of the two nymphs in the poem, which is far more complex and obscure than its popularity would suggest, seems to represent the world of the senses and therefore to resemble Hérodiade as the nurse wants her to be, while the purer of the two may well symbolise the world of the intellect and therefore resemble Hérodiade as she herself wants to be. And since the faun of the title is able to master neither of them one might hazard the conclusion that Mallarmé is again presenting his own predicament of a poet who is moving away from the material world but who has not yet reached the immaterial world and who is consequently incapable of dealing satisfactorily with either. 'L'Après-midi d'un faune' could in fact be said to be not unlike 'Le Pitre châtié' which indeed could well be an alternative title for it. Mallarmé's still unresolved dilemma is the theme of yet another poem, 'Brise marine', written in May 1865 when he was about to begin 'L'Après-midi d'un faune'. The birth of his daughter Geneviève in November 1864 led him this time to link together, perhaps rather oddly, the difficulties of family life and those of trying to write 'ideal' poetry. He is again seized with the longing to escape from his problems, no doubt in the literary as well as the physical sense, but as in 'Le vierge, le vivace et le bel aujourd'hui', he refuses to yield to temptation. If, however, the cold light of reason, Hérodiade's 'clair regard de diamant', is turned upon the problem of the existence of the ideal world, the conclusion which must inevitably be reached is that beyond the real world there lies nothing but an empty void. Yet if, at the same time, despite the evidence of the senses, the conviction is firmly held that the ideal world does exist, then the inescapable conclusion is that it somehow lies hidden in this empty void. It is this belief that is expressed symbolically in 'Sainte', written in December 1865 and first entitled 'Sainte Cécile jouant sur l'aile d'un chérubin', in which the material image of a viola has faded from a stained glass window but has been replaced, as shafts of light radiate from the setting sun, by the immaterial images, first of the feathers of an angel's wing and then, in a second mutation, by the strings of a harp on which the fingers of Saint Cecilia can create a new kind of music.

Mallarmé's desire to do likewise and to find inspiration in the immaterial rather than the material world is only implicit in this poem, but in the three sonnets, 'Tout Orgueil fume-t-il du soir', 'Surgi de la croupe et du bond' and 'Une dentelle s'abolit', which are in fact three parts of a single poem, he describes much more directly a spell of intense creative effort, lasting from dusk till dawn, which ends, however, in failure. In the first sonnet the flame of fresh inspiration does not leap, as he had hoped, from the ashes of his abandoned, traditional forms of poetry; no fertile liquid fills the vase which, in the second sonnet, he imagines himself to be; his creative faculty, symbolised by the two images of a bed and a mandolin in the third sonnet, fails to give birth to a new kind of poetry.

Although published only in 1887 these sonnets date from twenty years before as far as their initial inspiration is concerned and Mallarmé's correspondence at this period helps to explain his ideas. In July 1866 he wrote to his friend Cazalis: 'Je suis mort et ressuscité avec la clef de pierreries de ma dernière cassette spirituelle. A moi maintenant de l'ouvrir en l'absence de toute impression empruntée'. This idea of not being dependent on impressions made by material objects, of being truly creative in the sense of no longer merely describing something which already exists, is further developed in another letter written in May 1867 where Mallarmé contends that he has become simply a kind of prism through which the light from the ideal world is refracted and transformed: 'Je suis maintenant impersonnel... une aptitude qu'a l'univers spirituel à se voir et à se développer à travers ce qui fut moi'. It is worth noting that in both these letters, especially the first one, Mallarmé, either by accident or design, makes of himself a Christ-like figure which further makes it clear that he is concerned not with the material but with the immaterial world.

By 1867 therefore, when he was still only twenty-five years old, Mallarmé knew what it was that he wanted to do as a poet, and his goal was to remain unchanged throughout the rest of his life. Twenty years later he said, in a famous phrase, that his aim was to describe not a real flower, but the ideal flower that can never be found in this world: 'l'absente de tous bouquets'. This point is made even more clearly in another phrase written at the same time in which Mallarmé contends that the whole purpose of poetry is to create ideal forms, unsullied by any contact with reality: 'la notion pure, sans la gêne d'un proche ou concret rappel'.

Despite the obvious difficulty of using language for truly creative purposes and not for what he scornfully called 'reporting', Mallarmé soon acquired a boundless confidence in his ability to achieve his goal. It was in 1868 that he wrote the first version of the sonnet 'Ses purs ongles', thirteen lines of which emphasise time after time the total emptiness of a room which is then transformed, in the final line, into a vast, starlit universe. This is clearly symbolic of Mallarmé's ideas about conjuring up ideal forms from the empty void, but in view of the fact that the poem was first entitled 'Sonnet allégorique de lui-même' it seems clear that it is also symbolic of Mallarmé's confidence that his period of sterility is now over and that he has indeed become 'an instrument through which the spiritual world can be made perceptible and can develop'.

This same confidence is apparent in the sonnet 'Quand l'ombre menaça de la fatale loi' which, although published only in 1883, undoubtedly dates from this period fifteen years before. There is the same sudden transition from the dark and funereal confines of a closed room to the vast expanse of a starlit universe, although it occurs this time much earlier in the poem at the beginning of the second quatrain. And when, towards the end of the poem, Mallarmé describes the earth as having been transformed into a shining star by the birth of his genius, one is reminded of the star of Bethlehem so that there is the same implied analogy between the poet and Christ that can be detected in the two phrases quoted above from his letters to Cazalis in 1866.

Since Mallarmé was so convinced of his new found ability to reveal a whole new universe of ideal forms, one might have expected from him a sudden burst of poetic activity as from 1868. The very opposite was, however, the case, for he wrote no new poems for the next five years until the death of Théophile Gautier inspired 'Toast funèbre' in 1873. Then came a further silence of three years broken by an invitation to write the 'Tombeau de Poe' in 1876 and, in the following year, on the occasion of the death of the wife of one of his friends, by the composition of 'Sur les bois oubliés'. Then came another long silence of seven years before 'Prose – pour des Esseintes' in 1884.

The explanation of this extraordinary slowing down in Mallarmé's poetic production seems to be twofold. In the first place he was working on what he called his *Grand Œuvre*. The term is a significant one in that it means not only a *magnum opus* in the sense that any writer might use it of his major work, it also means, as Mallarmé himself said in a letter to Cazalis in May 1867, the philosopher's stone sought by the alchemists, the secret formula by which base metal can be transmuted into gold – an obvious symbol of what Mallarmé was seeking to achieve in his poetry. The second reason for Mallarmé producing so little lies in the very nature of this task, for to describe, or rather to create, in his poetry not a single real rose, for example, but the ideal quintessence of all roses meant that he was bound to engage in an inevitably slow and elaborate process of intense concentration and compression so as to instil the maximum significance into his lines. To acquire and perfect such a technique demands long practice and this was what Mallarmé spent much of his time doing in the years of virtual silence. He in fact referred to all his poems as mere preliminary studies, 'études en vue de mieux, comme on essaie les becs de sa plume avant de se mettre à l'œuvre'. This is particularly true of those poems which were first written between 1864 and 1868 but which were not published until much later, considerably modified in accordance with his new technique. 'Le Pitre châtié', for example, provides some excellent illustrations of the kind of processes Mallarmé applied to his poetry. In the first version the opening lines were:

> Pour ses yeux – pour nager dans ces lacs dont les quais
> Sont plantés de beaux cils qu'un matin bleu pénètre...

In the later version all this is shortened to just the two words: 'Yeux, lacs...', thus creating space for the extensive development of an analogy between the poet and the actor which was merely hinted at in the first version. Here again there is a good example of the extreme density of Mallarmé's language, for in order to emphasise this analogy, to create the illusion that he and the actor are one and the same person, he associates a noun in the third person with a verb in the first person:

> Yeux, lacs, avec ma simple ivresse de renaître
> Autre que l'histrion qui du geste évoquais...

The trilogy of the three sonnets, 'Tout Orgueil fume-t-il du soir', 'Surgi de la croupe et du bond' and 'Une dentelle s'abolit', first inspired, in all probability in 1866 and then compressed and condensed before being published twenty years later, furnish some equally good examples of Mallarmé's art of cramming a whole universe of meaning, connotation and overtone into a few lines of poetry. There are changing analogies between the poet on the one hand and, on the other, the sun, a fire, a vase, a bed and a mandolin. There are subtle links between these images, a sunless sky being like a hearth without a fire, a vase without a flower, a bedroom without a bed and a silent mandolin. There is a note of death and desolation in the first sonnet, giving way to an undertone of sexuality in the second sonnet, which links up with the notion of birth, or rather of failure to give birth, in the third sonnet.

Perhaps the best example of all of Mallarmé's extraordinary ability to achieve the maximum effect in his poems is provided by the sonnet 'Ses purs ongles'. Any other poet would no doubt have been satisfied simply with the visual image of an utterly empty room suddenly opening up on to the vastness of the universe, and would have been content with a purely arbitrary rhyme scheme. But Mallarmé was determined that the idea conveyed visually in the poem should be repeated auditively by the exclusive use of the two rhymes 'ix' and 'or', the first of which is the sound of the letter 'x', the generally accepted symbol of the unknown, while the principal meaning of the second word is 'gold', the equally accepted symbol of the ultimate ideal. Both are extremely difficult rhymes and it is an astonishing *tour de force* for Mallarmé to have accomplished this feat. He also applies his customary process of compression to the poem – his anguish is not merely symbolised by the onyx statuette, it actually becomes the statuette; it is not just the paper on which he has set down his thoughts which is burned, but the thoughts themselves; the carving round the mirror and the mirror itself are mentioned only after they have already been described; the constellation of the Great Bear is not specified but is merely implicit in the reference to seven stars in the northern sky. This last point illustrates another aspect of Mallarmé's technique. An inevitable result of his ambition to do something more than describe tangible objects in the real world was that he tended increasingly to avoid direct references to such objects, preferring instead indirect allusions so as not to become too closely tied to reality. He felt that by this means he was actually creating a new constellation or a new flower lying half concealed within the poem: 'évoquer, dans une ombre exprès, l'objet tu, par des mots allusifs, jamais directs, se réduisant à du silence égal, comporte tentative proche de créer'. Many of his celebrated pronouncements on the purpose of his poetry constantly reiterate this point, such as the phrases already quoted about conjuring up 'la notion pure, sans la gêne d'un proche ou concret rappel' and about banishing into oblivion the shape of any real flower so that out of the void thus created could emerge the ideal flower that has no existence here on earth: 'Je dis: une fleur! et, hors de l'oubli où ma voix relègue aucun contour, en tant que quelque chose d'autre que les calices sus, musicalement se lève, idée même et suave, l'absente de tous bouquets'. He felt that the reader too should participate in this creative act and his objection to the Parnassian poets of the time was that they dealt with things too openly and too clearly: 'Ils retirent aux esprits cette joie délicieuse de croire qu'ils créent'. He made the same point in his well-known reply to the enquiry on literature conducted by the journalist Jules Huret in 1891: '*Nommer* un objet c'est supprimer les trois quarts de la jouissance du poème qui est faite de deviner peu à peu: le *suggérer*, voilà le rêve'.

While Mallarmé was perfecting this technique of compression, connotation, allusion and suggestion he was also reflecting on his basic belief that beyond this world an ideal world lies concealed, that infinity can be conjured up from the void. An obvious variation on this theme is that eternal life can come from death, that when a man is reduced to nothingness he can nevertheless live on in some way. This is no doubt why Mallarmé was attracted to the elegy, especially the elegy addressed to creative artists since they are examples of men who have died and yet who live on in their work. 'Toast funèbre', 'Le Tombeau de Poe' and 'Sur les bois oubliés' are not therefore purely occasional poems; although inspired by particular circumstances they are also closely related to Mallarmé's ideas. Just as he had proclaimed, in 'Quand l'ombre menaça' that his own genius would shine out more and more strongly down the centuries, so he claims, on Gautier's behalf, in 'Toast funèbre', that 'le splendide génie éternel n'a pas d'ombre', and, on Poe's behalf, in the 'Tombeau de Poe' that death has finally changed the poet into his true self, the eternal artist rather than the mortal man. Even in 'Sur les bois oubliés', although the poem is not addressed to a creative artist, emphasis is laid on the power of the word which is able to transcend death and bring the dead wife back from the grave.

Apart from these elegies Mallarmé was no doubt working at his *Grand Œuvre* from 1868 to 1884, and he also busied himself preparing 'L'Après-midi d'un faune' for publication in 1876 as well as taking on, for financial reasons, a number of other commitments such as editing a few numbers of a fashion magazine, *La Dernière Mode*, at the end of 1874, compiling an English grammar book, *Les Mots Anglais*, published in 1877 and adding to it a manual dealing with classical mythology, *Les Dieux Antiques*, published in 1880. Poetically speaking however he remained virtually silent for seventeen years until the publication, in January 1885 in *La Revue Indépendante,* of the extraordinary poem bearing the enigmatic title 'Prose' and dedicated to Floressas des Esseintes, the decadent hero of J K Huysmans' novel *A Rebours* which had just been published. For the over-refined tastes of des Esseintes the prose poem was the supreme literary form and it may be for this reason that Mallarmé, tongue in cheek, decided to call what is clearly, for all other readers, a poem in verse: 'Prose – pour des Esseintes'. Otherwise, however, the poem has a serious purpose, for it is a renewed declaration by Mallarmé, parallel to his confident, and even over-confident declaration seventeen years before, in 'Quand l'ombre menaça de la fatale loi', that his period of silence is now over, that he has now perfected his technique of conjuring up the ideal world, that his *Grand Œuvre* is at last to see the light of day.

But while Mallarmé was writing 'Prose' he was also yielding to the charms of Méry Laurent, the former mistress of the painter Edouard Manet who had died in April 1883. In fact at precisely the time 'Prose' was published, in January 1885, Mallarmé wrote to a friend enclosing a copy of a poem which he had presumably just completed, 'Quelle soie aux baumes de temps' the theme of which is the very reverse of his promise, in 'Prose', to at last set down on 'eternal parchment' his vision of the ideal world. He is now more than willing to exchange the rôle of poet for that of lover and to abandon his dreams of fame and glory in favour of the pleasures to be found in Méry's company. Similarly in 'Victorieusement fui le suicide beau' and in 'M'introduire dans ton histoire', with its deliberately equivocal opening line, he is only too delighted to give up burning the midnight oil working at his *Grand Œuvre* in favour of spending his nights with Méry. Once again therefore, in 1885 as in 1868, Mallarmé's optimistic declaration of faith in his ability to attain his ideal world is followed by a failure to do so. This time however, instead of lapsing into silence, he wrote and published a number of poems about Méry Laurent, reflecting the successive stages of the relationship between them which gradually changed from an extreme sensuality (the opening lines of 'Dame sans trop d'ardeur', once the symbolism of the rose opening its petals to receive the precious tears has been understood, must be among the most specifically erotic ever to have been written) to the almost fraternal tenderness, which was to endure until the poet's death, of 'O si chère de loin'.

Although these love poems are of considerable merit and are typically Mallarmean in their technique (see the notes on pp. 172–174), they clearly mark a turning away from the ideal world towards the world of reality. Not surprisingly Mallarmé experienced the inevitable reaction and felt a certain tinge of regret that he had failed to carry out his promise, a regret that was all the more acute because he was now well over forty and his chances of taking up his task once more and carrying it through to completion were becoming increasingly slim. Even in one of the Méry Laurent poems, 'Mes bouquins refermés', his thoughts turn towards the non-existent breast of a legendary Amazon despite the presence of the voluptuous charms of his mistress, thus signalling a momentary longing for the ideal rather than the real. But his regret is most strongly expressed in the elegy he wrote to Wagner, who had died in 1883, for the *Revue Wagnerienne* in 1886, which he entitled 'Hommage' rather than 'Tombeau' and in which he recognised that the composer had succeeded where the poet had failed and that the ideas metaphorically gathering dust in the corners of his mind (and no doubt literally in the corners of his writing desk) would now never see the light of day.

By 1893 however, Mallarmé had recovered some of his optimism in the sonnet at first entitled 'Toast' (since it was recited as such to his friends at a literary banquet) and later 'Salut', where he once more re-affirmed his faith in his goal. But this time he defines the latter in no more than the vaguest terms as 'n'importe ce qui valut le blanc souci de notre toile'. Instead of the overwhelming confidence of 'Quand l'ombre' and 'Prose' that he will reach his goal, he now feels uncertain whether what awaits him is success or failure, or some lonely limbo between the two. Despite its title and its apparently light-hearted tone, 'Salut' can be classed as a kind of elegy in that it is really a reflection on the fate which awaits Mallarmé after his death. The same is true of the sonnet published two years later in 1895, 'A la nue accablante tu' which is pervaded by an uncertainty of a rather different kind. In this poem Mallarmé is in doubt not about his ultimate fate, but about the true worth of what he has achieved. He now seems convinced that his work will never survive, but in a moment of unusually profound pessimism he also wonders whether this will mean the loss to posterity not of a great poet, but of a mere versifier.

Uncertain and despondent though he may have felt at times during these years, Mallarmé nevertheless recovered sufficiently from his pessimism on occasions to write elegies to Baudelaire in 1895, to Verlaine in 1897 and to Vasco da Gama in 1898. This last poem, 'Au seul souci de voyager' was written to celebrate the 400th anniversary of da Gama's voyage to India, but Mallarmé also saw in the great explorer's persistence in sailing onwards into the unknown against all odds an image of his own pursuit of the ideal world, despite disappointments and setbacks.

This acceptance of the 'souci de voyager' as a substitute for the more ambitious 'souci d'arriver' can also be perceived in what is no doubt the most original and hermetic of all Mallarmé's works, *Un coup de dés jamais n'abolira le hasard*, published in 1897. So as to indicate the structure of this fairly lengthy and extremely complex piece of prose made up of some 650 words covering 21 pages Mallarmé uses different kinds of lettering. The main clause, printed in bold capitals, is interrupted after 'jamais' by a subordinate clause in smaller capitals which, in turn, is interrupted by a long and intricate passage in ordinary roman type. Only after these two parentheses does the verb 'n'abolira' appear and it too is followed by a long parenthesis in italics before the object of the verb, 'le hasard', makes its appearance. A final qualifying clause is then introduced, at first in italics and then in roman type, to bring the work to a close. In addition to this visual indication of the relative emphasis to be given to the various sections of the text, *Un coup de dés* also has a pictorial element. The words and sentences are sparingly distributed across the comparatively large area of the double page, which Mallarmé uses as his 'frame' instead of the single page, so that the lines of print, sometimes trailing across the paper like a drawing of the wake of a ship, sometimes grouped together like black dots on white dice, and sometimes more widely scattered like black stars in a white sky, reinforce the three kinds of imagery which dominate *Un coup de dés*, much as the sounds 'ix' and 'or' complement the imagery of 'Ses purs ongles'.

There is indeed a close relationship between these two works, although the optimism implicit in the constellation rising triumphantly out of the empty room in 1868 has given way, almost thirty years later, to a calm resignation implicit in a similar constellation quietly presiding over a catastrophic shipwreck. This is the wreck of Mallarmé's hope of ever attaining his goal, but he finds a twofold consolation for not having succeeded in producing his *Grand Œuvre*; firstly in the thought that, even if he had launched this work upon the world, it could still have passed unnoticed, for the fact of throwing a dice does not abolish the chance that the dice may not be seen; and secondly in the thought that, even if the dice is not thrown, even if the *Grand Œuvre* is not published, nevertheless the ideas that have gone into its making will themselves constitute a less obvious throw of the dice and may chance to survive. 'Toute Pensée émet un Coup de Dés' is the modestly optimistic conclusion, printed in appropriately modest lettering, of this extraordinarily original and complex work.

Now that almost a century has elapsed since Mallarmé wrote those words as the final line of *Un coup de dés*, the year before his death in 1898, it seems safe to say that the hope they express has been realised and that, even though he did not manage to complete and to publish his *Grand Œuvre* and thus give it a chance of survival, nevertheless the few works that he did publish, particularly his poems and *Un coup de dés* itself, have ensured him a place as one of the brightest stars in the great constellation of writers who make the late nineteenth century such a brilliant period in French literature.

FURTHER READING

Among numerous modern editions of Mallarmé's *Poésies* (the only collected edition of his poems prepared by him and published in 1899 shortly after his death) the following luxury edition deserves to be particularly recommended and should be consulted for its helpful introduction, its fairly extensive bibliography and its judicious commentaries on the poems which draw upon a wide range of the many and varied interpretations that have been offered:

> STÉPHANE MALLARMÉ, *Poésies*, textes présentés et commentés par Pierre Citron, Paris, Imprimerie Nationale, 1986.

A more accessible edition of the *Poésies* plus a substantial number of poems which Mallarmé left unpublished has recently appeared. It has useful notes and commentaries.

> MALLARMÉ, *Poésies*, Préface d'Yves Bonnefoy. Edition de Bertrand Marchal, Paris, NRF Gallimard, 1992.

The following edition, in the easily obtainable Classiques Garnier series, includes all the poetry plus a number of prose works and *Un coup de dés* along with an introduction, bibliography and notes:

> MALLARMÉ, *Œuvres*, textes établis avec chronologie, introduction, notes, choix de variantes et bibliographie par Yves-Alain Favre, Paris, Garnier, 1985.

These and other recent editions are indebted to the edition of Mallarmé's complete works published almost fifty years ago:

> STÉPHANE MALLARMÉ, *Œuvres complètes*, texte établi et annoté par Henri Mondor et G. Jean-Aubry, Paris, Gallimard, Bibliothèque de la Pléiade, 1945.

This edition is being superseded by a more recent edition of the complete works, of which only the first volume has so far been published:

> STÉPHANE MALLARMÉ, *Œuvres complètes, Vol.I, Poésies,* édition critique présenté par Carl Paul Barbier et Charles Gordon Millan, Paris, Flammarion, 1983.

There is a vast amount of critical work on Mallarmé. Among the most useful, for those who seek a basic understanding of his poems, are the following:

C. CHADWICK, *Mallarmé, sa pensée dans sa poésie*, Paris, Corti, 1962.

R. G. COHN, *Towards the poems of Mallarmé*, Los Angeles, University of California Press, 1965.

GARDNER DAVIES, *Les Tombeaux de Mallarmé*, Paris, Corti, 1950.

GARDNER DAVIES, *Vers une explication rationelle du coup de dés*, Paris, Corti, 1953 (2nd edition 1992).

ROSEMARY LLOYD, *Mallarmé, Poésies*, London, Grant & Cutler, 1984.

BERTRAND MARCHAL, *Lecture de Mallarmé*, Paris, Corti, 1985.

GUY MICHAUD, *Mallarmé*, Paris, Hatier 1971.

GUY MICHAUD, *Mallarmé*, translated by Marie Collins and Bertha Humez, London, Peter Owen, 1965 (from an earlier version of Michaud's study).

EMILIE NOULET, *Vingt poèmes de Stéphane Mallarmé*, Geneva, Droz, 1967.

A biography of Mallarmé in English has recently been published:

GORDON MILLAN, *Mallarmé: A Throw of The Dice: The Life of Stéphane Mallarmé*, London, Secker, 1994.

EARLY ASPIRATIONS
1862 – 1864

APPARITION

La lune s'attristait. Des séraphins en pleurs
Rêvant, l'archet aux doigts, dans le calme des fleurs
Vaporeuses, tiraient, de mourantes violes,
De blancs sanglots glissant sur l'azur des corolles.
– C'était le jour béni de ton premier baiser.
Ma songerie, aimant à me martyriser,
S'enivrait savamment du parfum de tristesse
Que même sans regret et sans déboire laisse
La cueillaison d'un Rêve au cœur qui l'a cueilli.
J'errais donc, l'œil rivé sur le pavé vieilli,
Quand, avec du soleil aux cheveux, dans la rue
Et dans le soir, tu m'es en riant apparue
Et j'ai cru voir la fée au chapeau de clarté
Qui jadis, sur mes beaux sommeils d'enfant gâté
Passait, laissant toujours de ses mains mal fermées
Neiger de blancs bouquets d'étoiles parfumées.

APPARITION

In the sad moonlight, weeping angels, holding violin
bows between their fingers in the calm of perfumed
flowers, drew, from the dying strings, pale tears
which flowed across the blue of the petals – it was
the sacred day of your first kiss. Recollecting in
my memory the exquisite pain of that moment
I subtly savoured the touch of sadness that, even
though there is no actual regret or distaste, the
realisation of a dream nevertheless leaves in the
heart that has transformed it into reality. So I
wandered along, my gaze fixed on the old paving
stones, when in the street at evening you suddenly
appeared before me, full of laughter with your blond
hair shining, and I thought I saw the fairy with the
halo of light who, in the blissful dreams of my happy
childhood, used to hover above me and sprinkle from
her gentle hands snow-white clusters of perfumed stars.

LES FENÊTRES

Las du triste hôpital, et de l'encens fétide
Qui monte en la blancheur banale des rideaux
Vers le grand crucifix ennuyé du mur vide
Le moribond sournois y redresse un vieux dos,

Se traîne et va, moins pour chauffer sa pourriture
Que pour voir du soleil sur les pierres, coller
Les poils blancs et les os de sa maigre figure
Aux fenêtres qu'un beau rayon clair veut hâler.

Et la bouche, fiévreuse et d'azur bleu vorace,
Telle, jeune, elle alla respirer son trésor,
Une peau virginale et de jadis! encrasse
D'un long baiser amer les tièdes carreaux d'or.

Ivre, il vit, oubliant l'horreur des saintes huiles,
Les tisanes, l'horloge et le lit infligé,
La toux; et quand le soir saigne parmi les tuiles
Son œil, à l'horizon de lumière gorgé,

Voit des galères d'or, belles comme des cygnes,
Sur un fleuve de pourpre et de parfums dormir
En berçant l'éclair fauve et riche de leurs lignes
Dans un grand nonchaloir chargé de souvenir!

Ainsi, pris du dégoût de l'homme à l'âme dure
Vautré dans le bonheur, où ses seuls appétits
Mangent, et qui s'entête à chercher dans cette ordure
Pour l'offrir à la femme allaitant ses petits,

THE WINDOWS

Tired of the dreary hospital and of the sickly smell
seeping through the dull whiteness of the curtains
towards the tall, solitary crucifix on the bare wall,
the dying man stealthily raises his weary body and
drags himself across to the window, not so much in
order to warm his decaying flesh, as to see the
sunlight on the stones, to press against the glass
his white beard and the bony cheeks of his thin face
that the clear bright sun seems anxious to bronze.
And his fevered lips, as thirsty for the blue sky as
they once were, in his younger days, for the first
taste, now long past, of love, leave upon the warm,
golden panes the mark of a long and bitter kiss.
Drunk with happiness he feels alive again, forgetting
the horror of the healing lotions, the medicines, the
ticking of the clock, the discomfort of the bed and
the painful cough; and when evening glows among
the roof tiles he sees, on the horizon filled with light,
golden galleons, as lovely as swans, moored on a broad
river of scented purple, their tawny, gleaming hulls
slowly swaying as if laden with memories.
In similar fashion, disgusted with the selfishness of men
wallowing in pleasure, interested only in satisfying their
appetites and persistently pursuing this sordid existence
to offer it to their wives suckling their children,

Je fuis et je m'accroche à toutes les croisées
D'où l'on tourne l'épaule à la vie, et, béni,
Dans leur verre, lavé d'éternelles rosées,
Que dore le matin chaste de l'Infini

Je me mire et me vois ange! et je meurs, et j'aime
– Que la vitre soit l'art, soit la mysticité –
A renaître, portant mon rêve en diadème,
Au ciel antérieur où fleurit la Beauté!

Mais, hélas! Ici-bas est maître: sa hantise
Vient m'écœurer parfois jusqu'en cet abri sûr,
Et le vomissement impur de la Bêtise
Me force à me boucher le nez devant l'azur.

Est-il moyen, ô Moi qui connaît l'amertume,
D'enfoncer le cristal par le monstre insulté
Et de m'enfuir, avec mes deux ailes sans plume
– Au risque de tomber pendant l'éternité?

I have fled from them and cling to all those windows
where one can turn one's back on life; and in their
glass, constantly washed by new-fallen dew and lit
by the golden light of the endless sky at dawn
I can see my reflection like that of an angel, and
I feel that I am dying and, through the medium of
art or of mystical experience, I want to be reborn,
wearing my dream like a diadem, in some better
land where beauty flourishes.
But alas, this earth below triumphs; haunted by it,
I am sickened even in this safe retreat and have to
shut out the animal smell of humanity, despite my
vision of the world above.
Is there any way, I wonder in my bitterness,
of breaking through the glass thus insulted
and of soaring upwards on my useless wings –
at the risk of plunging into eternal oblivion?

L'AZUR

De l'éternel azur la sereine ironie
Accable, belle indolemment comme les fleurs,
Le poète impuissant qui maudit son génie
A travers un désert stérile de Douleurs.

Fuyant, les yeux fermés, je le sens qui regarde
Avec l'intensité d'un remords atterrant,
Mon âme vide. Où fuir? Et quelle nuit hagarde
Jeter, lambeaux, jeter sur ce mépris navrant?

Brouillards, montez! Versez vos cendres monotones
Avec de longs haillons de brume dans les cieux
Que noiera le marais livide des automnes
Et bâtissez un grand plafond silencieux!

Et toi, sors des étangs léthéens et ramasse
En t'en venant la vase et les pâles roseaux,
Cher Ennui, pour boucher d'une main jamais lasse
Les grands trous bleus que font méchamment les oiseaux.

Encor! que sans répit les tristes cheminées
Fument, et que de suie une errante prison
Eteigne dans l'horreur de ses noires trainées
Le soleil se mourant jaunâtre à l'horizon!

– Le Ciel est mort. – Vers toi, j'accours! donne, ô matière
L'oubli de l'Idéal cruel et du Péché
A ce martyr qui vient partager la litière
Où le bétail heureux des hommes est couché,

THE SKY

The serene irony of the eternal sky, as indolently
lovely as flowers, overwhelms the impotent poet who
curses his genius amidst a sterile desert of sorrows.
But as I flee, with eyes closed, I can sense, with the
intensity of overwhelming remorse, the sky looking
into my empty soul. Where shall I flee? And what
dark night can I find to drag like ragged curtains
across this agonising scorn?
Rise up, fogs! Lift your dreary ash-grey rags of mist
towards the skies, so as to drown them in autumn's
damp gloom and build up a vast and silent ceiling!
Let lethargy crawl up from the banks of Lethe, bringing
with it mud and reeds to stop up relentlessly the great
slashes of blue sky cruelly made by the birds.
Still more! Let sluggish smoke rise from the chimneys
and a drifting prison of soot blot out, in its grim trails
of black, the yellowing sun dying on the horizon!
– The sky is dead. – I fling myself to the earth pleading
to be allowed to forget the ideal world and my feeling of
guilt at having abandoned the cruel struggle towards it.
I am a martyr who wants only to share the byre where
the human herd is contentedly gathered.

Car j'y veux, puisque enfin ma cervelle, vidée
Comme le pot de fard gisant au pied d'un mur,
N'a plus l'art d'attifer la sanglotante idée,
Lugubrement bâiller vers un trépas obscur...

En vain! L'Azur triomphe, et je l'entends qui chante
Dans les cloches. Mon âme, il se fait voix pour plus
Nous faire peur avec sa victoire méchante
Et du métal vivant sort en bleus angélus!

Il roule par la brume, ancien et traverse
Ta native agonie ainsi qu'un glaive sûr;
Où fuir dans la révolte inutile et perverse?
Je suis hanté. L'Azur! L'Azur! L'Azur! L'Azur!

Since my brain, as empty as an old jar of make-up lying
against a wall, no longer knows how to give to my ideas
the form they desperately long for, I want to drag my way
sadly and wearily towards an obscure death...
But my efforts are in vain; the sky triumphs and I can hear
its victorious clamour in the bells. O my soul, it has become
a voice so as to frighten us the more with its cruel victory
and it is springing from the living metal in brilliant carillons.
It thunders through the mist as strong as ever and pierces
your old wound like a sharp sword. Where can I flee
in my useless and perverse revolt? I am haunted by
the sky, the sky, the sky, the sky.

Las de l'amer repos où ma paresse offense
Une gloire pour qui jadis j'ai fui l'enfance
Adorable des bois de roses sous l'azur
Naturel, et plus las sept fois du pacte dur
De creuser par veillée une fosse nouvelle
Dans le terrain avare et froid de ma cervelle,
Fossoyeur sans pitié pour la stérilité,
– Que dire à cette Aurore, ô Rêves, visité
Par les roses, quand, peur de ses roses livides,
Le vaste cimetière unira les trous vides? –
Je veux délaisser l'art vorace d'un pays
Cruel, et, souriant aux reproches vieillis
Que me font mes amis, le passé, le génie,
Et ma lampe qui sait pourtant mon agonie,
Imiter le Chinois au cœur limpide et fin
De qui l'extase pure est de peindre la fin
Sur ses tasses de neige à la lune ravie
D'une bizarre fleur qui parfume sa vie
Transparente, la fleur qu'il a sentie, enfant,
Au filigrane bleu de l'âme se greffant.
Et, la mort telle avec le seul rêve du sage,
Serein, je vais choisir un jeune paysage
Que je peindrais encor sur les tasses, distrait.
Une ligne d'azur mince et pâle serait
Un lac, parmi le ciel de porcelaine nue,
Un clair croissant perdu par une blanche nue
Trempe sa corne calme en la glace des eaux,
Non loin de trois grands cils d'émeraude, roseaux.

Bitterly weary of doing nothing, for my idleness is an
insult to my dreams of literary glory which made me flee
the childish pleasures and delights of everyday life, and
still more weary of sticking to my firm resolve to spend
long hours of the night digging into the cold unyielding
earth of my brain, refusing to take pity on its sterility
(when the Day of Judgement dawns, when the dead rise from
their graves, leaving empty holes in the cemetery whose pale
roses of death will recoil before the roses of eternal life,
what shall I have to say about my dreams and ambitions?)
Tired of these fruitless efforts I want to abandon the
cruelly exacting poetry that I have been trying to write
and, with a sad smile of resignation at the reproaches
of my friends, the past, my genius and my lamp which has
been the witness of my desperate struggle, I want instead
to imitate the delicate, untroubled nature of Chinese art,
taking a serene pleasure in painting, on porcelain cups as
white as snow gleaming in the moonlight, the fading of some
strange flower whose perfume fills the artist's peaceful
life, the perfume which, as a child, he felt growing into
the eternal fabric of his soul. To live and die in this
fashion being the only sensible ambition of a wise man,
I shall serenely choose a pleasant landscape that, with
a tranquil mind, I will describe as if I too were painting
on cups. A pale, thin line of blue shall be a lake, amid the
sky of untinted porcelain; a clear crescent moon alongside
a white cloud shall dip one of its horns into the cool water,
not far from three tall reeds like emerald eyelashes.

LES FLEURS

Des avalanches d'or du vieil azur, au jour
Premier, et de la neige éternelle des astres
Jadis tu détachas les grands calices pour
La terre jeune encore et vierge de désastres,

Le glaïeul fauve, avec les cygnes au col fin,
Et ce divin laurier des âmes exilées
Vermeil comme le pur orteil du séraphin
Que rougit la pudeur des aurores foulées,

L'hyacinthe, le myrte à l'adorable éclair
Et, pareille à la chair de la femme, la rose
Cruelle, Hérodiade en fleur du jardin clair,
Celle qu'un sang farouche et radieux arrose!

Et tu fis la blancheur sanglotante des lys
Qui roulant sur des mers de soupirs qu'elle effleure
A travers l'encens bleu des horizons pâlis
Monte rêveusement vers la lune qui pleure!

Hosannah sur le cistre et dans les encensoirs,
Notre Dame, hosannah du jardin de nos limbes!
Et finisse l'écho par les célestes soirs,
Extase des regards, scintillement des nimbes!

O Mère qui créas en ton sein juste et fort,
Calices balançant la future fiole,
De grandes fleurs avec la balsamique Mort
Pour le poète las que la vie étiole.

FLOWERS

At the dawn of creation, from the floods of golden
light loosed by the eternal sky and from the undying
white brilliance of the stars, you drew flowers for
the newly made earth untouched by disaster;
the wild iris, among which glide swans with slender
necks, the divine laurel beloved of exiled souls,
whose rose colour is like the flesh of an angel as
he treads underfoot the blushing skies of dawn,
the hyacinth, the lovely white myrtle and the
cruel rose, so like a woman's flesh, the Salome
of the flowers in the sunlit garden, the one
that is savagely and splendidly bathed in blood.
And you made the sad whiteness of the lilies
which, echoing softly across oceans of sighs
and the smoky blue of fading horizons, reaches
dreamily towards the weeping moon.
Let us give praise, with our lutes and censers,
to mother nature; let us sing her praises from
the gardens here below and let these songs finish
in a heavenly twilight among the clear gaze of
angels and the gleam of their halos.
For it is you, Nature, who, from your kindly bosom,
have created these flowers, with their foretaste of
the future balm of death, for the weary poet who is
tired of life.

LE PITRE CHÂTIÉ

Yeux, lacs avec ma simple ivresse de renaître
Autre que l'histrion qui du geste évoquais
Comme plume la suie ignoble des quinquets,
J'ai troué dans le mur de toile une fenêtre.

De ma jambe et des bras limpide nageur traître,
A bonds multipliés, reniant le mauvais
Hamlet! c'est comme si dans l'onde j'innovais
Mille sépulcres pour y vierge disparaître.

Hilare or de cymbale à des poings irrité,
Tout à coup le soleil frappe la nudité
Qui pure s'exhala de ma fraîcheur de nacre,

Rance nuit de la peau quand sur moi vous passiez,
Ne sachant pas, ingrat! que c'était tout mon sacre,
Ce fard noyé dans l'eau perfide des glaciers.

THE TURNCOAT PUNISHED

Naïvely tempted to again write romantic verse about
women's eyes looking like pools, to be something other
than a writer of carefully rehearsed poetry, wielding
my pen in the murky light of my lamp like an actor
practising gestures with his feathered hat in the
sullen glare of the footlights, I tore up my vain
efforts and, as if the actor had burst through the
curtain into the auditorium or like a diver with feet
together and arms apart, I plunged time and again,
a traitor to my true vocation as much as the actor
abandoning his failed attempt to play Hamlet, into
the refreshing waters of lyric poetry, ready to turn
out thousands of lines though I knew they would
be tombstones beneath which my talent, untested
by true creative effort, would be buried.
The joyful golden disk of the sun however, like a
cymbal brandished aloft, suddenly struck my naked
swimmer's body, whose mother-of-pearl freshness
made me feel the rôle I had been playing was dark
and tainted, for, ungrateful creature that I was, I did
not realise that this was where my sacred talent lay,
in this carefully meditated poetry, this equivalent of
the actor's make-up that I had as if washed away in the
cool and treacherous waters of facile romantic verse.

SOUPIR

Mon âme vers ton front où rêve, ô calme sœur,
Un automne jonché de taches de rousseur,
Et vers le ciel errant de ton œil angélique
Monte, comme dans un jardin mélancolique,
Fidèle, un blanc jet d'eau soupire vers l'Azur!
– Vers l'Azur attendri d'Octobre pâle et pur
Qui mire aux grands bassins sa langueur infinie
Et laisse, sur l'eau morte où la fauve agonie
Des feuilles erre au vent et creuse un froid sillon,
Se traîner le soleil jaune d'un long rayon.

ASPIRATION

Towards your calm brow, Muse, where the russet leaves
of autumn lie, and towards the unattainable heaven of
your angel's eyes, my faithful soul aspires like a white
fountain of water in a melancholy garden reaching up
towards the sky; towards the pitying sky of October,
pale and clear, whose infinite weariness is reflected
in the round ponds and which lets the yellow sun, with
its slanting rays, drag itself across the lifeless water
furrowed by the icy wake of the faded, dying leaves
as they drift in the wind.

Le vierge, le vivace et le bel aujourd'hui
Va-t-il nous déchirer avec un coup d'aile ivre
Ce lac dur oublié que hante sous le givre
Le transparent glacier des vols qui n'ont pas fui!

Un cygne d'autrefois se souvient que c'est lui
Magnifique mais qui sans espoir se délivre
Pour n'avoir pas chanté la région où vivre
Quand du stérile hiver a resplendi l'ennui.

Tout son col secouera cette blanche agonie
Par l'espace infligée à l'oiseau qui le nie,
Mais non l'horreur du sol où le plumage est pris.

Fantôme qu'à ce lieu son pur éclat assigne,
Il s'immobilise au songe froid de mépris
Que vêt parmi l'exil inutile le Cygne.

Will this be the day, dawning lively and lovely, when
my creative talent will at last soar upwards, like a
bird breaking free, with one wild blow of its wing,
from the frozen waters of a lonely lake, beneath whose
frosty surface lies a transparent glacier made up of
successive days of failure.

A former day remembers that it too was once like a
magnificent swan, but that, not having sung in time of its
true home, the sky, before the numbing onset of sterile and
wintry inactivity, it was only with a feeling of hopeless-
ness that it finally dragged itself away across the ice.

But the new day, though it will shake from its swan-like
neck the deathly frost that settles on a bird which denies
its true element, will not free itself from the horror of
the ice in which it is gripped.

Thus it becomes a ghost condemned to this fate by the
purity of its ideals and it settles into stillness as it thinks
coldly and disdainfully of the previous day, covering it
with scorn in its useless exile.

THE REJECTION
OF THE MATERIAL WORLD
1864 – 1865

HÉRODIADE
SCÈNE
La Nourrice – Hérodiade

                    N.

Tu vis! ou vois-je ici l'ombre d'une princesse?
A mes lèvres tes doigts et leurs bagues et cesse
De marcher dans un âge ignoré...

                    H.
                              Reculez.

Le blond torrent de mes cheveux immaculés
Quand il baigne mon corps solitaire le glace
D'horreur, et mes cheveux que la lumière enlace
Sont immortels. O femme, un baiser me tûrait
Si la beauté n'était la mort...
                    Par quel attrait
Menée et quel matin oublié des prophètes
Verse, sur les lointains mourants, ses tristes fêtes,
Le sais-je? tu m'as vue, ô nourrice d'hiver
Sous la lourde prison de pierres et de fer
Où de mes vieux lions traînent les siècles fauves
Entrer, et je marchais, fatale, les mains sauves,
Dans le parfum désert de ces anciens rois:
Mais encore as-tu vu quels furent mes effrois?
Je m'arrête rêvant aux exils, et j'effeuille,
Comme près d'un bassin dont le jet d'eau m'accueille,
Les pâles lys qui sont en moi, tandis qu'épris,
De suivre du regard les languides débris
Descendre, à travers ma rêverie, en silence,
Les lions, de ma robe écartent l'indolence
Et regardent mes pieds qui calmeraient la mer.
Calme, toi, les frissons de ta sénile chair,
Viens et ma chevelure imitant les manières

HERODIADE
SCENE BETWEEN THE NURSE AND HERODIADE

N.

Are you still alive or is it the ghost of a princess that
I see? Let me kiss the rings on your fingers and persuade
you not to persist in remaining in another world...

H.

Stand back. Even my pure blond hair, when it streams
down my shoulders and bathes my lonely body, chills me with
horror, and yet my hair, glinting with shafts of light, does not
belong to this mortal world. A kiss from you would kill me,
were it not that my beauty is such that I am already
dead to others... What mysterious force, I wonder, and what
dawning light unknown to other seekers, sheds over the distant
horizons its painful yet joyful rays? You have seen me, nurse,
in the winter months, enter the grim prison of stone walls and
iron bars where my lions recall past centuries of savage cruelty
and I walked there, on the verge of death and yet unharmed,
alone amid the scent of these old rulers of the animal kingdom.
But did you realise how frightened I was? I used to stand,
dreaming of other worlds, as if near a welcoming fountain
cascading into a pond, and strip the leaves from the pale lilies
of my romantic imagination, while the lions would watch,
fascinated, the torn leaves drift silently away through my
dreams and would push aside the heavy folds of my dress and
watch my feet which were steady enough to calm the sea itself.
So you too must calm the trembling of your aged limbs, and
since my hair is so like a wild lion's mane that it frightens

Trop farouches qui sont votre peur des crinières,
Aide-moi, puisqu'ainsi tu n'oses plus me voir,
A me peigner nonchalamment dans un miroir.

N.

Sinon la myrrhe gaie en ses bouteilles closes,
De l'essence ravie aux vieillesses de roses,
Voulez-vous, mon enfant, essayer la vertu
Funèbre?

H.

Laisse là ces parfums! ne sais-tu
Que je les hais, nourrice, et veux-tu que je sente
Leur ivresse noyer ma tête languissante?
Je veux que mes cheveux qui ne sont pas des fleurs
A répandre l'oubli des humaines douleurs,
Mais de l'or, à jamais vierge des aromates,
Dans leur éclairs cruels et dans leurs pâleurs mates,
Observent la froideur stérile du métal,
Vous ayant reflétés, joyaux du mur natal,
Armes, vases depuis ma solitaire enfance.

N.

Pardon! L'âge effaçait, reine, votre défense
De mon esprit pâli comme un vieux livre ou noir...

H.

Assez! Tiens devant moi ce miroir.

O miroir!
Eau froide par l'ennui dans ton cadre gelée
Que de fois et pendant des heures, désolée
Des songes et cherchant mes souvenirs qui sont
Comme des feuilles sous ta glace au trou profond,
Je m'apparus en toi comme une ombre lointaine,
Mais, horreur! des soirs, dans ta sévère fontaine,

you and that you no longer dare to look at me as I am,
come and help me to comb it quietly in front of a mirror.

N.

If you do not want to take from its closed bottles
the lively scent of myrrh, will you then, my child,
try the sadder perfume culled from dying roses?

H.

Put aside those perfumes. Do you not know, nurse, that
I hate them and would you have me let their heady aroma
make my tired brain swim? My hair has nothing to do
with flowers bringing forgetfulness of human griefs, but
is more like gold with its cruel gleam and pale sheen
free from any taint of perfume, and I want it to keep
the sterile metallic coldness of the weapons and vases,
adorning the walls of my birthplace, that it has
reflected ever since my lonely childhood.

N.

Forgive me, queen; old age made my fading memory,
as dry and dusty as an old book, forget that you had
banned these perfumes...

H.

Say no more but hold this mirror up in front of me.
O mirror, pool of water frozen by weariness into your
frame, how often and for how many long hours, saddened
by my dreams and searching for memories that are like
leaves sunk deep beneath your icy surface, did I gaze
at my shadowy reflection; but, to my horror, when evening
came, peering into your limpid water, I realised how bare

J'ai de mon rêve épars connu la nudité!
Nourrice, suis-je belle?

N.

Un astre, en vérité

Mais cette tresse tombe...

H.

Arrête dans ton crime

Qui refroidit mon sang vers sa source, et réprime
Ce geste, impiété fameuse: ah! conte-moi
Quel sûr démon te jette en le sinistre émoi,
Ce baiser, ces parfums offerts et, le dirai-je?
O mon cœur, cette main encore sacrilège,
Car tu voulais, je crois, me toucher, sont un jour
Qui ne finira pas sans malheur sur la tour...
O jour qu'Hérodiade avec effroi regarde!

N.

Temps bizarre en effet, de quoi le ciel vous garde!
Vous errez, ombre seule et nouvelle fureur,
Et regardant en vous précoce avec terreur;
Mais toujours adorable autant qu'une immortelle,
O mon enfant, et belle affreusement et telle
Que...

H.

Mais n'allais-tu pas me toucher?

N.

J'aimerais

Etre à qui le destin réserve vos secrets.

H.

Oh! tais-toi!

N.

Viendra-t-il parfois?

and meaningless my vague dreams were.
Nurse, am I beautiful?

N.

You are indeed supremely so; but this lock of hair is falling...

H.

Take your hand away. So outrageously impious a gesture
would be a crime chilling my blood right to its very source.
Tell me what persistent demon is causing you to make these
sinister emotional gestures. Your kiss, the perfumes you
offered and, if I can bear to say it, your sacrilegious hand
(for I believe you wanted to touch me) all this suggests that the
day will not end without some disaster occurring within these
walls, a day which Herodiade contemplates with fear and
trembling.

N.

These are indeed strange times that we are living through and
may heaven protect you from them. You wander to and fro like
a lonely ghost or some latter-day fury, gazing with terror into
your own soul, young though you are. But you are nonetheless
as adorable as a goddess, my child, and frighteningly
beautiful, so much so that...

H.

Were you about to touch me again?

N.

I wish I were the man in whom you are destined to confide
your secrets.

H.

You must not say such things.

N.

Will he come, I wonder?

H.

Etoiles pures,

N'entendez pas!

N.

Comment, sinon parmi d'obscures
Epouvantes, songer plus implacable encore
Et comme suppliant le dieu que le trésor
De votre grâce attend! et pour qui, dévorée
D'angoisses, gardez-vous la splendeur ignorée
Et le mystère vain de votre être?

H.

Pour moi.

N.

Triste fleur qui croît seule et n'a pas d'autre émoi
Que son ombre dans l'eau vue avec atonie.

H.

Va, garde ta pitié comme ton ironie.

N.

Toutefois expliquez: oh! non, naïve enfant,
Décroîtra, quelque jour, ce dédain triomphant.

H.

Mais qui me toucherait, des lions respectée?
Du reste, je ne veux rien d'humain et, sculptée,
Si tu me vois les yeux perdus au paradis,
C'est que je me souviens de ton lait bu jadis.

N.

Victime lamentable à son destin offerte!

H.

You heavenly stars, do not listen to her.

N.

How can one imagine, save in some dark and terrifying
way, the god whom your precious beauty is awaiting,
a being still more implacable than you and yet who
would be your suitor? Consumed as you are by anguished
thoughts, for whom are you keeping the unknown splendour
and the vain mystery of your being?

H.

For myself.

N.

It is a sad flower that grows alone and knows no feeling
other than the dull reaction caused by the sight of its
own shadowy reflection in the water.

H.

You may keep your pity as well as your irony.

N.

But why not explain to me, my poor child, whether
or not one day your proud disdain will lessen.

H.

But who would dare to come close to me when the lions
themselves respect me? Moreover, I want no contact
with the human world, and if you see me, standing like
a statue, gazing with a lost look in my eyes towards
some paradise, it is when I am looking back to the
distant days when you suckled me.

N.

You are like some pitiful victim awaiting her fate.

H.

Oui, c'est pour moi, pour moi, que je fleuris, déserte!
        Vous le savez, jardins d'améthyste, enfouis
Sans fin dans de savants abîmes éblouis,
Ors ignorés, gardant votre antique lumière
Sous le sombre sommeil d'une terre première,
Vous, pierres où mes yeux comme de purs bijoux
Empruntent leur clarté mélodieuse, et vous
Métaux qui donnez à ma jeune chevelure
Une splendeur fatale et sa massive allure!
Quant à toi, femme née en des siècles malins
Pour la méchanceté des antres sibyllins,
Qui parles d'un mortel! selon qui, des calices
De mes robes, arome aux farouches délices,
Sortirait le frisson blanc de ma nudité,
Prophétise que si le tiède azur d'été,
Vers lui nativement la femme se dévoile,
Me voit dans ma pudeur grelottante d'étoile,
Je meurs!
        J'aime l'horreur d'être vierge et je veux
Vivre parmi l'effroi que me font mes cheveux
Pour, le soir, retirée en ma couche, reptile
Inviolé sentir en la chair inutile
Le froid scintillement de ta pâle clarté
Toi qui te meurs, toi qui brûles de chasteté,
Nuit blanche de glaçons et de neige cruelle!
Et ta sœur solitaire, ô ma sœur éternelle
Mon rêve montera vers toi: telle déjà,
Rare limpidité d'un cœur qui le songea,
Je me crois seule en ma monotone patrie
Et tout, autour de moi, vit dans l'idolâtrie
D'un miroir qui reflète en son calme dormant
Hérodiade au clair regard de diamant...

H.

Yes, it is for myself and myself alone that my beauty
flowers in solitude. You can understand me, clusters
of amethyst, buried for all eternity in deep and dazzling
abysses, unknown seams of gold, conserving your age-old
gleam in the dark slumber of the earth's earliest rocks,
precious stones from which my eyes, like pure jewels,
borrow their radiant light, and metals which give to my
youthful hair its captivating brilliance and heavy waves.
As for you, nurse, born in a malicious age to make wicked
prophecies like some Delphic oracle, you who talk of a
mortal suitor, you, according to whom, from the petals
of my dress, like a perfume redolent of animal pleasures,
my naked body should emerge white and trembling, you
may prophesy instead that if even the warm summer sky, to
which women ordinarily reveal themselves, were to see me
pure and trembling in my shameful nakedness, I would die.
I love the horror of remaining a virgin and I want to live
with the fear which my own hair causes me so that, at night,
I can lie on my bed like some inviolate serpent and feel,
on my unused body, the cold gleam of the moon's pale light,
the dying moon, the shining symbol of chastity, above the
night landscape of ice and cruelly cold snow. And so, being
your sister in solitude, my dream will drift up towards you,
my eternal, heavenly sister. With the strange clarity of one
who has foreseen this happening, I already feel that I am alone
in my native land which no longer means anything to me, and
everything around me is subordinate to my intense
concentration on a mirror which reflects, in its calm untroubled
depths, Herodiade with her crystal-clear gaze...

O charme dernier, oui! je le sens, je suis seule.

                        N.
Madame, allez-vous donc mourir?

                        H.
                        Non, pauvre aïeule,
Sois calme, et, t'éloignant, pardonne à ce cœur dur,
Mais avant, si tu veux, clos les volets, l'azur
Séraphique sourit dans les vitres profondes,
Et je déteste, moi, le bel azur!
                        Des ondes
Se bercent et, là-bas, sais-tu pas un pays
Où le sinistre ciel ait des regards haïs
De Vénus qui, le soir, brûle dans le feuillage:
J'y partirais.
                        Allume encore, enfantillage
Dis-tu, ces flambeaux où la cire au feu léger
Pleure parmi l'or vain quelque pleur étranger
Et…

                        N.
        Maintenant?

                        H.
                Adieu.
                        Vous mentez, ô fleur nue
De mes lèvres.
                        J'attends une chose inconnue
Où peut-être, ignorant le mystère et vos cris
Jetez-vous les sanglots suprêmes et meurtris
D'une enfance sentant parmi les rêveries
Se séparer enfin ses froides pierreries.

At last, the supreme bliss of feeling that I am alone.

N.

Madam, are you then about to die?

H.

No, my poor old nurse, be calm and, as you leave me,
forgive my harshness; but first, I beg you, close the
shutters, for the heavenly blue sky is smiling far
beyond the windows and now I hate the loveliness of
the sky.

I can hear the sound of the sea and I wonder if, some-
where beyond, there may not be a land where the sky
has a sinister look, hated by Venus ardent with love
among the trees at evening; that is the land I shall seek.
Will you also yield to what you may think is a childish
whim and light the candles whose slow flame melts the
wax which falls like strange tears on the useless gold of
the holder and...

N.

And now?

H.

Farewell.

My lips lied when they said that my beauty was
flowering for myself alone.

I am awaiting something unknown, or perhaps, though
unaware what this mysterious fate is, and equally
unaware of the reason for the cries of anguish they
have uttered, my lips are giving the last painful sobs of a
childhood which is feeling its vague, uncertain dreams
crystallising at last into something sharper and clearer.

L'APRÈS-MIDI D'UN FAUNE

Le Faune

Ces nymphes, je les veux perpétuer.
                                            Si clair,
Leur incarnat léger, qu'il voltige dans l'air
Assoupi de sommeils touffus.
                                    Aimai-je un rêve?
Mon doute, amas de nuit ancienne, s'achève
En maint rameau subtil, qui, demeuré les vrais
Bois mêmes, prouve, hélas! que bien seul je m'offrais
Pour triomphe la faute idéale de roses.
Réfléchissons...
                          ou si les femmes dont tu gloses
Figurent un souhait de tes sens fabuleux!
Faune, l'illusion s'échappe des yeux bleus
Et froids, comme une source en pleurs, de la plus chaste
Mais, l'autre tout soupirs, dis-tu qu'elle contraste
Comme brise du jour chaude dans ta toison!
Que non! par l'immobile et lasse pâmoison
Suffoquant de chaleurs le matin frais s'il lutte,
Ne murmure point d'eau que ne verse ma flûte
Au bosquet arrosé d'accords; et le seul vent
Hors des deux tuyaux prompt à s'exhaler avant
Qu'il disperse le son dans une pluie aride,
C'est, à l'horizon pas remué d'une ride,
Le visible et serein souffle artificiel
De l'inspiration, qui regagne le ciel.

O bords siciliens d'un calme marécage
Qu'à l'envi des soleils ma vanité saccage,
Tacite sous les fleurs d'étincelles, CONTEZ

A SATYR AWAKES

The satyr

Those nymphs, I want to make them live for ever. The rosy
tint of their flesh was so clear and light that it seems still
to be floating in the drowsy air after my heavy sleep.

Perhaps it was no more than a dream? The scene, as I vaguely
remember it, now that my eyes are open, was set in a tangle of
slender branches which, since they still surround me as real
trees, prove, alas, that I was all alone and merely imagined
that I had triumphed over the rosy blushes of nymphs. Let us
reflect further on this matter... Were the women I am talking
of merely the creation of my fevered senses? I remember being
captivated by the limpid gaze that flowed like a spring from
the cool blue eyes of the purer of the two; while the other,
full of sighs, I recollect that she, in contrast, was like
the warm breeze of a summer's day on my body. And
yet no such dreams could have been inspired by my
surroundings, for among the still and silent lassitude
induced by the heat as it suffocates the freshness of the
invading morning, there is no murmur of water other than
the sound of my flute sprinkling its harmonies over the
bushes; and the only breeze, as far as the motionless horizon,
is the clear and serene artificial breeze of my breath rising
in the air as it is quickly exhaled from my two pipes before
scattering its notes like dry rain. Let then the fringes of
this calm Sicilian marsh, lying silent beneath the sparkling
radiance of the sun which envies the way in which I, in my
musician's vanity, plunder them, let them tell what happened:

"Que je coupais ici les creux roseaux domptés
Par le talent; quand, sur l'or glauque de lointaines
Verdures dédiant leur vigne à des fontaines,
Ondoie une blancheur animale au repos:
Et qu'au prélude lent où naissent les pipeaux .
Ce vol de cygnes, non! de naïades se sauve
Ou plonge..."
                Inerte, tout brûle dans l'heure fauve
Sans marquer par quel art ensemble détala
Trop d'hymen souhaité par qui cherche le *la*:
Alors m'éveillerai-je à la ferveur première,
Droit et seul, sous un flot antique de lumière,
Lys! et l'un de vous tous pour l'ingénuité.

Autre que ce doux rien par leur lèvre ébruité,
Le baiser, qui tout bas des perfides assure,
Mon sein, vierge de preuve, atteste une morsure
Mystérieuse, due à quelque auguste dent;
Mais, bast! arcane tel élut pour confident
Le jonc vaste et jumeau dont sous l'azur on joue:
Qui, détournant à soi le trouble de la joue
Rêve, dans un solo long, que nous amusions
La beauté d'alentour par des confusions
Fausses entre elle-même et notre chant crédule;
Et de faire aussi haut que l'amour se module
Evanouir du songe ordinaire de dos
Ou de flanc pur suivis avec mes regards clos,
Une sonore, vaine et monotone ligne.

Tâche donc, instrument des fuites, ô maligne
Syrinx, de refleurir aux lacs ou tu m'attends!
Moi, de ma rumeur fier, je vais parler longtemps
Des déesses; et par d'idolâtres peintures,

"that I was gathering the hollow reeds which my talented
fingers tame, when, on the green and gold background of
some distant vines, dipping their leaves towards the water,
there appeared a white gleam of flesh in repose; and that,
at the sound of my pipes as I slowly tuned them, this
flight of swans, no, of nymphs, suddenly flew away
or plunged into the water..."

But now all is still in the burning heat of noon, with
no sign as to how all these ardently desired nymphs
managed to escape while I was tuning my pipes; must
I then return to my original fevered state, standing here
alone, beneath the sunlight endlessly pouring down, with
one of these pure white lilies as a symbol of my innocence.

As well as any sweet, ephemeral kiss, tacitly assuring
constancy from the inconstant, that their lips may have
promised, my chest, previously unsullied by any mark,
now bears a mysterious scar, the toothmark of some divine
creature. But I must say no more of this secret that I
confided to the long twin reeds which I play beneath the
sky and which, taking upon themselves the troubled emotions
which my cheek betrays, endeavour, in a long solo, to
delight the lovely countryside by pretending that it was
the source of our foolish song and to draw, from the dreams
of white bodies that my closed eyes pursued, a quiet and
plaintive line of melody soaring upwards as high as love itself.

Try then instrument of escape, enchanted flute, to flower
afresh beside the lake where your reeds await me. Proud of my
music, I shall long sing of these goddesses and, worshipping
them in imagination, I shall unloose the dresses their shadows

A leur ombre enlever encore des ceintures;
Ainsi, quand des raisins j'ai sucé la clarté,
Pour bannir un regret par ma feinte écarté,
Rieur, j'élève au ciel d'été une grappe vide
Et, soufflant dans ses peaux lumineuses, avide
D'ivresses, jusqu'au soir je regarde au travers.

O nymphes, regonflons des SOUVENIRS divers.

"Mon œil, trouant les joncs, dardait chaque encolure
Immortelle, qui noie en l'onde sa brûlure
Avec un cri de rage au ciel de la forêt;
Et le splendide bain de cheveux disparaît
Dans les clartés et les frissons, ô pierreries!
J'accours; quand, à mes pieds, s'entrejoignent (meurtries
De la langueur goûtée à ce mal d'être deux)
Des dormeuses parmi leurs seuls bras hasardeux;
Je les ravis, sans les désenlacer, et vole
A ce massif, haï par l'ombrage frivole,
De roses tarissant tout parfum au soleil,
Où notre ébat au jour consumé soit pareil."
Je t'adore, courroux des vierges, ô délice
Farouche du sacré fardeau nu qui se glisse
Pour fuir ma lèvre en feu buvant, comme un éclair
Tressaille! la frayeur secrète de la chair:
Des pieds de l'inhumaine au cœur de la timide
Que délaisse à la fois une innocence, humide
De larmes folles ou de moins tristes vapeurs.
"Mon crime, c'est d'avoir, gai de vaincre ces peurs
Traîtresses, divisé la touffe échevelée
De baisers que les dieux gardaient si bien mêlée:
Car, à peine j'allais cacher un rire ardent
Sous les replis heureux d'une seule (gardant
Par un doigt simple, afin que sa candeur de plume
Se teignît à l'émoi de sa sœur qui s'allume,

wear; and when I have sucked the flesh from the grapes so as
to banish any lingering regret, already largely dispelled by my
substitute pleasure, I shall laughingly lift up the remains of
the bunch and blowing into the translucent grapeskins, waiting
to fall asleep, I shall look through them at the summer sky till
evening falls. Let us similarly breathe new life into our various
memories of these nymphs: *"My eyes, peering through
the reeds, lit upon their immortally beautiful breasts as,
with a cry of rage at the canopy of trees above them,
they plunged into the water away from my burning gaze;
and their superb flowing hair disappeared amid glints and
flickers of light like so many jewels. I ran forward and
suddenly stumbled on two nymphs, their limbs entwined,
tightly locked in the loving and languorous embrace of
a couple oblivious to all others. I seized them, without
separating them, and fled to this bed of roses, whose
perfume evaporates in the sun and over which no cooling
shade ever passes, so that we should make love with a
similar consuming ardour."* I adored their virginal anger,
the wild delight of feeling my precious naked burden slip
to one side, trying to escape my lips which, as fiery as
flickering lightning flashes, tasted the secret fears of
their bodies, from the feet of the cruel one to the breast
of the timid one, as their innocence abandoned them both,
bathed in wild tears or in the heat of other passions
less sad. *"My mistake was to have been carried away
by my success in overcoming these treacherous fears
and to have separated these intertwined bodies that the
gods obviously wished to keep together; for scarcely had
I begun to expend my delight and my love on the joyful,
sinuous body of one of them (restraining with the lightest*

La petite, naïve et ne rougissant pas):
Que de mes bras, défaits par de vagues trépas,
Cette proie, à jamais ingrate, se délivre
Sans pitié du sanglot dont j'étais encore ivre."

Tant pis! vers le bonheur d'autres m'entraîneront
Par leur tresse nouée aux cornes de mon front:
Tu sais, ma passion, que, pourpre et déjà mûre,
Chaque grenade éclate et d'abeilles murmure;

Et notre sang, épris de qui va le saisir,
Coule pour tout l'essaim éternel du désir.
A l'heure ou ce bois d'or et de cendres se teinte
Une fête s'exalte en la feuillée éteinte:
Etna! c'est parmi toi visité de Vénus
Sur ta lave posant ses talons ingénus,
Quand tonne un somme triste ou s'épuise la flamme.
Je tiens la reine!

    O sûr châtiment...
         Non, mais l'âme
De paroles vacante et ce corps alourdi
Tard succombent au fier silence de midi:
Sans plus il faut dormir en l'oubli du blasphème,
Sur le sable altéré gisant et comme j'aime
Ouvrir ma bouche à l'astre efficace des vins!

Couple, adieu; je vais voir l'ombre que tu devins.

of touches the smaller of the two, naïve and unblushing,
so that her fresh purity should be affected by the ardour
of her sister's mounting passion) when, from my arms,
become weak and numb in some strange way, my ungrateful
prey escaped, heedless of the sobs that still filled my throat."

What does it matter? Others will lead me towards happiness,
binding their hair to the horns on my brow. I know that the
summer fruits now red and ripe are murmuring at the approach
of the bees and, in similar fashion, my hot blood, in love with
the first comer, surges for the whole eternal swarm of
passionate desires. At this hour, when the surrounding
woods are coloured gold and red, a bright light
leaps up among the burnt foliage: it is Etna, as Venus
walks barefoot on its lava flanks and the volcano murmurs
sadly in its sleep or gives out a last flicker of light.
Have I then the queen of love herself within my grasp?
Certain punishment would result. No, I am dreaming;
my soul, empty of words, and my weary body are at last
yielding to the profound noontide silence. I must
fall asleep now, forgetful of my attempts, and, lying
on the dry sand, as I love to do, open my lips to the
healing balm of wine. Farewell nymphs, I shall now see
the shadows that you have become.

BRISE MARINE

La chair est triste, hélas! et j'ai lu tous les livres
Fuir! là-bas fuir! Je sens que les oiseaux sont ivres
D'être parmi l'écume inconnue et les cieux!
Rien, ni les vieux jardins reflétés par les yeux
Ne retiendra ce cœur qui dans la mer se trempe
O nuits! ni la clarté déserte de ma lampe
Sur le vide papier que la blancheur défend
Et ni la jeune femme allaitant son enfant.
Je partirai! Steamer balançant ta mâture,
Lève l'ancre pour une exotique nature!

Un Ennui, désolé par les cruels espoirs,
Croit encore à l'adieu suprême des mouchoirs!
Et peut-être les mâts, invitant les orages,
Sont-ils de ceux qu'un vent penche sur les naufrages
Perdus, sans mâts, sans mâts, ni fertiles ilôts...
Mais, ô mon cœur, entends le chant des matelots!

SEA BREEZE

Both the flesh and the spirit weary me; I am no longer
in love and I have read all my books. I long to get away,
to flee from this world to where the birds are wild with
joy to be flying across unknown seas and skies. Nothing
shall hold me back from my heart's desire to plunge deep
into the sea and to vanish into the night; neither the old
gardens I see around me, nor the unbroken circle of light
from my lamp, falling on the blank sheet of paper and its
forbidding whiteness, nor my wife suckling her child. I shall
abandon everything and board a steamer with swaying masts
setting off for some exotic land. For such is my weariness,
overwhelmed by disappointed hopes, that I still cherish the
illusion that one can really escape, that handkerchiefs can
wave in a truly final farewell. Even though these masts
may perhaps run into storms so that my dreams of escape
will lead only to the shipwreck of my hopes, instead of to the
welcoming island I visualise, my heart still finds it hard to
resist the idea of escape and the appeal of sailors' songs.

THE REVELATION
OF THE IDEAL WORLD
1865 – 1868

SAINTE

A la fenêtre recélant
Le santal vieux qui se dédore
De sa viole étincelant
Jadis avec flûte ou mandore,

Est la Sainte pâle, étalant
Le livre vieux qui se déplie
Du Magnificat ruisselant
Jadis selon vêpre ou complie:

A ce vitrage d'ostensoir
Que frôle une harpe par l'Ange
Formée avec son vol du soir
Pour la délicate phalange

Du doigt que, sans le vieux santal
Ni le vieux livre, elle balance
Sur le plumage instrumental,
Musicienne du silence.

SAINT CECILIA

In the old stained-glass window, the fading gilt of her
sandalwood viola now scarcely visible, although once it
sparkled beside a flute or a mandolin, sits the pale figure
of Saint Cecilia, the patron saint of music. Open on her
lap lies an old breviary which once also glowed with light
at the evening services of vespers and compline.
So she sits in this altar window, brushed by the rays of
the setting sun as if by the wing of the angel of dusk.
These rays resemble not only the feathers of a wing, but
also the strings of a harp lying beneath the delicate joints
of Saint Cecilia's fingers so that, although the sandalwood
viola and the old breviary have faded away, she nevertheless
has the means of making music, of drawing sound from
silence.

I

Tout Orgueil fume-t-il du soir,
Torche dans un branle étouffée
Sans que l'immortelle bouffée
Ne puisse à l'abandon surseoir!

La chambre ancienne de l'hoir
De maint riche mais chu trophée
Ne serait pas même chauffée
S'il survenait par le couloir.

Affres du passé nécessaires
Agrippant comme avec des serres
Le sépulcre de désaveu,

Sous un marbre lourd qu'elle isole
Ne s'allume pas d'autre feu
Que la fulgurante console.

I

Just as the evening sun sets proudly behind the clouds,
like a torch swung round and extinguished, without the
immortal beauty of the sunlit clouds being able to persuade
it not to disappear, so the poet is firm in his proud resolve
to abandon the kind of poetry, immortal yet insubstantial,
that he has so far written.
If, as the heir to a rich but outmoded tradition, he were
to return to his former style, he would find it like a cold,
unwelcoming room.
The destruction of his past poetry was a necessary though
painful act and the agony he felt is symbolised by the
claw-like feet of a console table gripping the hearth where,
in a gesture of disavowal, he has burned his poems.
But any hope that a new kind of poetry would rise from this
sepulchre of his dead verse is disappointed, for beneath the
heavy marble top, standing out in stark and tomb-like isolation,
there is no other light than the cold gleam of the gilded table
legs standing in the empty fireplace.

II

Surgi de la croupe et du bond
D'une verrerie éphémère
Sans fleurir la veillée amère
Le col ignoré s'interrompt.

Je crois bien que deux bouches n'ont
Bu, ni son amant ni ma mère,
Jamais à la même Chimère,
Moi, sylphe de ce froid plafond!

Le pur vase d'aucun breuvage
Que l'inexhaustible veuvage
Agonise mais ne consent,

Naïf baiser des plus funèbres!
A rien expirer annonçant
Une rose dans les ténèbres.

II

Surging up from its rounded base and rising flank a fragile
glass vase suddenly stops short, lacking the flower which
should prolong its line; similarly my painful night-long
creative struggle has failed to bear fruit.
I wonder whether I myself really exist, whether my mother
and her lover ever created me, whether they ever drank from
the same loving-cup, whether the latter was an illusion
so that I, in consequence, am no more than an insubstantial
sylph imprisoned within the confines of this cold room.
The vase, without the presence of any fertilising liquid, is
condemned to a kind of eternal, barren widowhood and finally
dies; but even in its death throes it can only breathe out a
dying, virginal kiss which in no way heralds the birth of a
rose in the shadows of the night.

III

Une dentelle s'abolit
Dans le doute du Jeu suprême
A n'entr'ouvrir comme un blasphème
Qu'absence éternelle de lit.

Cet unanime blanc conflit
D'une guirlande avec la même,
Enfui contre la vitre blême
Flotte plus qu'il n'ensevelit.

Mais, chez qui du rêve se dore
Tristement dore une mandore
Au creux néant musicien

Telle que vers quelque fenêtre
Selon nul ventre que le sien,
Filial on aurait pu naître.

III

A lace curtain becomes invisible as it is pierced by the
doubtful half-light of dawn when the sun rises to play its
part in the celestial game of the stars rolling through
the sky. As the light grows stronger it reveals that there
is no bed in the room, that the whole purpose of the latter's
existence is thus denied.
The white curtains, swirling about and inter-twining with
each other as they are blown against the glass of the window,
pale in the morning sun, merely float in the air and, being
of lace, do not conceal the interior of the room.
But, whereas in the room, bathed in the light of the rising
sun, there is no bed, no place of procreation, in the mind of
the poet, bathed in the light of his dream of achieving
greatness, the creative faculty is present but dormant, like
a silent mandolin from whose rounded, belly-like shape he had
hoped he would emerge as a new kind of poet soaring beyond
the confines of the room.

Ses purs ongles très haut dédiant leur onyx,
L'Angoisse, ce minuit, soutient, lampadophore,
Maint rêve vespéral brûlé par le Phénix
Que ne recueille pas de cinéraire amphore

Sur les crédences au salon vide: nul ptyx
Aboli bibelot d'inanité sonore
(Car le Maître est allé puiser des pleurs au Styx
Avec ce seul objet dont le Néant s'honore).

Mais proche la croisée au nord vacante, un or
Agonise selon peut-être le décor
Des licornes ruant du feu contre une nixe,

Elle, défunte nue en le miroir, encor
Que, dans l'oubli fermé par le cadre, se fixe
De scintillations sitôt le septuor.

The uplifted fingers of an onyx statuette, whose twisted
body symbolises the poet's anguish, hold up, at this mid-
night hour, the candle-flame in which the poet, a Phoenix
among men, has burned the products of his evening's labours.
There is no urn on the sideboard in the empty room to collect
the ashes of these failed dreams, nor even a sea-shell, for
this trivial, empty object in which the sound of the sea can
be heard, this symbol of the emergence of something from
nothing, has been removed by the master of the room who has
sorrowfully decided to end his life as a poet.
But near to the window open to the north stands a gilt-framed
mirror on which carved unicorns, in the dying light of the
candle, seem to be charging a water-nymph whose naked body
has sunk beneath the lake-like surface of the glass. Then in the
emptiness of this mirror, enclosed by its frame, appears the
symbol of infinity, a glittering constellation of seven stars.

Quand l'ombre menaça de la fatale loi
Tel vieux Rêve, désir et mal de mes vertèbres,
Affligé de périr sous des plafonds funèbres
Il a ployé son aile indubitable en moi.

Luxe, ô salle d'ébène où, pour séduire un roi
Se tordent dans leur mort des guirlandes célèbres,
Vous n'êtes qu'un orgueil menti par les ténèbres
Aux yeux du solitaire ébloui de sa foi.

Oui, je sais qu'au lointain de cette nuit, la Terre
Jette d'un grand éclat l'insolite mystère,
Sous les siècles hideux qui l'obscurcissent moins.

L'espace à soi pareil qu'il s'accroisse ou se nie
Roule dans cet ennui des feux vils pour témoins
Que s'est d'un astre en fête allumé le génie.

When failure threatened to destroy my persistent desire and
deep-rooted longing to write great poetry, saddened at the
thought of not attaining this ambitious goal, my dream of
glory, though never ceasing to exist, instead of taking wing,
became withdrawn and confined.

Now, however, the whole luxurious ebony vault of the sky
is open to me. Celebrated constellations, like garlands fit
for a king, twist and turn as their life ebbs away. Yet these
stars are no more than pin-points of light, whose vanity is
shown up by the surrounding darkness, in the eyes of the
solitary genius dazzled by his new-found belief.

For now I know that far into the night the earth is flinging
a strange and mysterious shaft of light whose brilliance will
only be increased by the passing centuries.

The universe, whether expanding or contracting, is there for
the sole purpose of rolling tiny specks of light through the
vast stretches of darkness so as to throw into greater relief
the dazzling star that the earth has become now that it has
been set alight by the birth of a genius.

ELEGIES I
1873 – 1877

TOAST FUNÈBRE

O de notre bonheur, toi, le fatal emblème!

Salut de la démence et libation blème,
Ne crois pas qu'au magique espoir du corridor
J'offre ma coupe vide où souffre un monstre d'or!
Ton apparition ne va pas me suffire:
Car je t'ai mis, moi-même, en un lieu de porphyre.
Le rite est pour les mains d'éteindre le flambeau
Contre le fer épais des portes du tombeau:
Et l'on ignore mal, élu pour notre fête
Très simple de chanter l'absence du poète,
Que ce beau monument l'enferme tout entier.
Si ce n'est que la gloire ardente du métier,
Jusqu'à l'heure commune et vile de la cendre,
Par le carreau qu'allume un soir fier d'y descendre,
Retourne vers les feux du pur soleil mortel!

Magnifique, total et solitaire, tel
Tremble de s'exhaler le faux orgueil des hommes.
Cette foule hagarde! elle annonce: Nous sommes
La triste opacité de nos spectres futurs.
Mais, le blason des deuils épars sur de vains murs
J'ai méprisé l'horreur lucide d'une larme,
Quand, sourd même à mon vers sacré qui ne n'alarme,
Quelqu'un de ces passants, fier, aveugle et muet,
Hôte de son linceul vague, se transmuait
En le vierge héros de l'attente posthume.
Vaste gouffre apporté dans l'amas de la brume
Par l'irascible vent des mots qu'il n'a pas dits,
Le néant à cet Homme aboli de jadis:
'Souvenirs d'horizons, qu'est-ce, ô toi, que la Terre?'
Hurle ce songe; et, voix dont la clarté s'altère,
L'espace a pour jouet le cri: 'Je ne sais pas!'

ELEGY ON THE DEATH OF THEOPHILE GAUTIER

You are the fateful symbol of the happiness that awaits us.

For you must not think that it is in the fond hope of seeing
you return to this world that I empty my golden goblet, with
some strange creature engraved on it, in a vain and foolish
salute and celebration. I know that you will not reappear in
response to my toast, for I myself helped to place you within
the marble tomb and observed the ritual by which our hands
extinguished against its heavy iron doors a symbolic flame;
and I know full well, having been chosen to celebrate in a few
simple lines of verse, the death of the poet, that within this
splendid tomb lies all that remains of him. All, that is, except
the glorious brilliance of his trade as a poet which, until that
day when all is reduced to dust and ashes, will project back
towards the stars, through the pane of glass lit up by the proudly
setting sun, a pure and earthly shaft of light.

You have gone to your death fearlessly, concealing nothing,
asking for no help, in a way in which other men, with their
falseness and vanity, are afraid to die. These ordinary mortals
huddled together in fear, well know that, dull and lacklustre
in life, they are equally so in death. On seeing the symbols
of mourning spread over bare walls, I spurned the awful thought
of shedding tears at the passing of a man of this kind, deaf
even to my aspiring poetry which is meaningless to him. Vain,
blind and dumb, wrapped in some nondescript shroud, he
awaited what the new life after death was to bring him.
But such a man is nothing more than a vast, empty space,
whirled away into the mists of eternity by the angry tempest
of the words he has failed to use. When the void flings at this
relic of what was once a man, as if in a dream, the question:
'From your memories of your past life, what is the earth like?',
the answer, tossed about through space like a toy, in a voice

Le Maître, par un œil profond, a, sur ses pas,
Apaisé de l'éden l'inquiète merveille
Dont le frisson final, dans sa voix seule, éveille
Pour la Rose et le Lys, le mystère d'un nom.
Est-il de ce destin rien qui demeure, non?
O vous tous, oubliez une croyance sombre.
Le splendide génie éternel n'a pas d'ombre.
Moi, de votre désir soucieux, je veux voir,
A qui s'évanouit, hier, dans le devoir
Idéal que nous font les jardins de cet astre,
Survivre pour l'honneur du tranquille désastre
Une agitation solennelle par l'air
De paroles, pourpre ivre et grand calice clair,
Que, pluie et diamant, le regard diaphane
Resté là sur ces fleurs dont nulle ne se fane,
Isole parmi l'heure et le rayon du jour!

C'est de nos vrais bosquets déjà tout le séjour,
Où le poète pur a pour geste humble et large
De l'interdire au rêve, ennemi de sa charge:
Afin que le matin de son repos altier,
Quand la mort ancienne est comme pour Gautier
De n'ouvrir pas les yeux sacrés et de se taire,
Surgisse, de l'allée ornement tributaire,
Le sépulcre solide où gît tout ce qui nuit,
Et l'avare silence et la massive nuit.

growing increasingly faint, is the cry: 'I do not know'.
The master poet, however, thanks to his penetrating gaze,
has, in the course of his journey on earth, stilled the
disquiet of the marvellous flowers whose death inspired,
in his unique voice, a mysterious new existence for the
rose and the lily in the realm of the word. Is there
nothing that remains of this achievement? Let any such
sombre thoughts be forgotten; radiant and eternal genius
cannot be dimmed. Sharing the desire of you all I want to
see Gautier, who departed from us yesterday in the midst
of his high ambition to immortalise earthly flowers, survived,
in honour of his tranquil death, by the solemn waving in the
air, not of flowers, but of words, describing the wild red
roses and tall white lilies on which, like rain and sparkling
sunlight, his clear gaze fell, ensuring that they should never
die and that they should be for ever sheltered from the passing
hours and days.

It is within the pages of books that our earthly flowers find
their true home, and the pure poet's humble yet important
task is to exclude, from this their final resting place, that
dreamy vagueness which is the chief danger he has to combat.
If this is achieved, then when the poet too has gone to his
final resting place, when inevitable death decrees that, as in
the case of Gautier, the god-like eyes must close and the voice
be stilled, only the massive tomb rising up in ornamental tribute
from the cemetery path will contain that which can harm him,
stony silence and utter darkness.

LE TOMBEAU D'EDGAR POE

Tel qu'en Lui-même enfin l'éternité le change,
Le Poète suscite avec un glaive nu
Son siècle épouvanté de n'avoir pas connu
Que la mort triomphait dans cette voix étrange!

Eux, comme un vil sursaut d'hydre oyant jadis l'ange
Donner un sens plus pur aux mots de la tribu
Proclamèrent très haut le sortilège bu
Dans le flot sans honneur de quelque noir mélange.

Du sol et de la nue hostiles, ô grief!
Si notre idée avec ne sculpte un bas-relief
Dont la tombe de Poe éblouissante s'orne,

Calme bloc ici-bas chu d'un désastre obscur,
Que ce granit du moins montre à jamais sa borne
Aux noirs vols du blasphème épars dans le futur.

ELEGY TO EDGAR ALLAN POE

Transformed at last into his true self by death, the
poet pricks, as with a naked sword, the conscience of
his contemporaries, horrified at not having recognised
that the strange quality of his voice was due to his
approaching death.
The public, like a monstrous multi-headed hydra, on
hearing this angelic voice giving a purer meaning to
the language of mortal men, loudly proclaimed that its
bewitching quality resulted from his shameful drunkenness.
How bitter a struggle between earthly creatures and a
divine spirit. If I cannot sculpt it into a bas-relief
to decorate Poe's magnificent tomb, which lies like a
meteorite fallen to earth after some mysterious cosmic
disaster, may the granite from which it is made at least
put an end to any foul attacks on the honour of the poet
that may await him in future years.

(Pour votre chère morte, son ami)
2 novembre 1877

'Sur les bois oubliés quand passe l'hiver sombre
Tu te plains, ô captif solitaire du seuil,
Que ce sépulcre à deux qui fera notre orgueil
Hélas! du manque seul des lourds bouquets s'encombre.

Sans écouter minuit qui jeta son vain nombre,
Une veille t'exalte à ne pas fermer l'œil
Avant que dans les bras de l'ancien fauteuil
Le suprême tison n'ait éclairé mon ombre.

Qui veut souvent avoir la Visite ne doit
Par trop de fleurs charger la pierre que mon doigt
Soulève avec l'ennui d'une force défunte.

Ame au si clair foyer tremblante de m'asseoir,
Pour revivre il suffit qu'à tes lèvres j'emprunte
Le souffle de mon nom murmuré tout un soir.'

(For your dear dead wife, from her friend)
2 November 1877

'When the dark days of winter keep you penned indoors
alone, forgetful of the woods, you complain that the
grandiose tomb in which both of us will one day lie,
seems all the more cumbersome through the lack of
masses of flowers.
Midnight has sounded its twelve strokes in vain, for
your long vigil urges you not to close your eyes until,
within the arms of the chair that once was mine, my
ghost has appeared, lit by the dying light of the fire.
If you wish me to return from the grave you must not
burden with too many flowers the tombstone that I push up
with the weary fingers of one whose strength has failed.
I am a soul longing to sit beside the bright hearth and
for me to thus live again all I need is to hear from your
lips the murmur of my name repeated throughout the night'.

RENEWED RESOLVE
1884

PROSE

   pour des Esseintes

Hyperbole! de ma mémoire
Triomphalement ne sais-tu
Te lever, aujourd'hui grimoire
Dans un livre de fer vêtu:

Car j'installe, par la science,
L'hymne des cœurs spirituels
En l'œuvre de ma patience,
Atlas, herbiers et rituels.

Nous promenions notre visage
(Nous fûmes deux je le maintiens)
Sur maints charmes de paysage,
O sœur, y comparant les tiens.

L'ère d'autorité se trouble
Lorsque, sans nul motif, on dit
De ce midi que notre double
Inconscience approfondit

Que, sol des cent iris, son site,
Ils savent s'il a bien été,
Ne porte pas de nom que cite
L'or de la trompette d'Eté.

Oui, dans une île que l'air charge
De vue et non de visions
Toute fleur s'étalait plus large
Sans que nous en devisions.

Telles, immenses, que chacune
Ordinairement se para
D'un lucide contour, lacune,
Qui des jardins la sépara.

PROSE

> *for des Esseintes*

A splendid, hyperbolic language, to match my vision
of the ideal world, has not yet succeeded in springing
triumphantly from my mind where it still lies, like a
secret cipher in an iron-bound book.
For my patient task is to give intellectual form to
emotional and spiritual aspirations, just as voyages
of discovery are noted in atlases, the growth of
flowers in studies of plants and the transcendental
quality of religions in books of ritual ceremonies.
We wandered together, I and this form of expression
I had in mind, through the ideal world, comparing its
charms to those of my companion, to see if the one
yet matched the other.
But my long-standing confidence is shaken when
people jealously contend that this sunlit land
which the two of us, forgetful of all else,
are exploring, this land of a hundred irises,
whose whereabouts they claim they would be
bound to know if it really existed, has no name
that has been generally proclaimed and can there-
fore be presumed not to exist.
But we maintain that it does exist, that, on an
island which we have really seen and not just
imagined, every flower was larger than life so
that we were struck dumb with admiration.
They were so heavenly in their grandeur that
each was permanently surrounded by a halo
of light that clearly distinguished it from the
flowers of earthly gardens.

Gloire du long désir, Idées
Tout en moi s'exaltait de voir
La famille des iridées
Surgir à ce nouveau devoir,

Mais cette sœur sensée et tendre
Ne porta son regard plus loin
Que sourire et, comme à l'entendre
J'occupe mon antique soin.

Oh! sache l'Esprit de litige,
A cette heure où nous nous taisons,
Que de lis multiples la tige
Grandissait trop pour nos raisons

Et non comme pleure la rive,
Quand son jeu monotone ment
A vouloir que l'ampleur arrive
Parmi mon jeune étonnement

D'ouïr tout le ciel et la carte
Sans fin attestés sur mes pas,
Par le flot même qui s'écarte,
Que ce pays n'exista pas.

L'enfant abdique son extase
Et docte déjà par chemins
Elle dit le mot: Anastase!
Né pour d'éternels parchemins,

Avant qu'un sépulcre ne rie
Sous aucun climat, son aïeul,
De porter ce nom: Pulchérie!
Caché par le trop grand glaïeul.

This was the glorious culmination of what I had
longed for, those ideal flowers I had sought,
and my heart leaped within me to see the whole
family of irises rise up in their turn at the
thought of my accepting the task of revealing
their existence.
But my companion, my wise and tender muse,
merely looked at me smilingly, and, as if
hearing her utter a warning, I am still
persisting in my long and careful study.
Let those who launch accusations against me
know therefore that, if we are silent at the
present time, it is because the stems of the
countless lilies we saw exceeded our ability
to comprehend them, and not because this ideal
world did not exist, as is plaintively alleged by
those earthbound creatures who persistently and
insincerely amuse themselves by demanding that
I tell of the splendour of what I have seen when
I am still overwhelmed by my initial wonderment
at hearing the sky above and the earth below bear
witness to their existence as I explore this promised
land, like a prophet before whom the sea has divided
to let me pass.
But now the poet has recovered from his ecstasy and,
having already learned much from his explorations,
his muse gives him the word of command: 'Rise to
your task', and urges him to set down what he has
seen in eternal poetry, before death, which time
must ultimately bring to all men, laughs in triumph
at seeing the ideal beauty perceived by the poet
going with him to the grave and being overgrown
and concealed by earthly flowers.

POEMS TO MÉRY LAURENT
1885 – 1888

Quelle soie aux baumes de temps
Où la Chimère s'exténue
Vaut la torse et native nue
Que, hors de ton miroir, tu tends!

Les trous de drapeaux méditants
S'exaltent dans notre avenue:
Moi, j'ai ta chevelure nue
Pour enfouir mes yeux contents.

Non! La bouche ne sera sûre
De rien goûter à sa morsure
S'il ne fait, ton princier amant,

Dans la considérable touffe
Expirer, comme un diamant,
Le cri des Gloires qu'il étouffe.

What silken flag symbolising the illusory balm of posthumous fame, that gradually dying chimera, is worth the loosely waving cloud of your hair, as, sitting in front of your mirror, you comb it back from your head.

The motionless flags hoisted high on their masts in the avenue pierce holes in the sky; but I have your unbound hair in which to plunge my contented gaze. My lips cannot be sure of savouring to the full the kisses they give unless your princely lover finally stifles his dreams of glory, burying them like a diamond in the great mass of your hair.

Victorieusement fui le suicide beau
Tison de gloire, sang par écume, or, tempête!
O rire si là-bas une poupre s'apprête
A ne tendre royal que mon absent tombeau.

Quoi! de tout cet éclat pas même le lambeau
S'attarde, il est minuit, à l'ombre qui nous fête
Excepté qu'un trésor présomptueux de tête
Verse son caressé nonchaloir sans flambeau,

La tienne si toujours le délice! la tienne
Oui seule qui du ciel évanoui retienne
Un peu de puéril triomphe en t'en coiffant

Avec clarté quand sur les coussins tu la poses
Comme un casque guerrier d'impératrice enfant
Dont pour te figurer il tomberait des roses.

Triumphantly abandoned now my one-time ambition to die
in splendour, spurred on by the thought of glory, with a
stormy sunset sky, streaked with red and gold, to symbolise
my passing. I can now view with amused detachment
the prospect of the regal draperies of the purple western
sky preparing to commemorate my death when there will
in fact be nothing to commemorate.
Of all this brilliant prospect not a shred remains among the
midnight shadows which welcome us, save that the proud gold
of your hair gleams coolly and softly beneath my caresses.
Your hair which has so long delighted me, your hair whose
glowing colour alone has captured some youthful, triumphant
vestige of the now faded sky, as you rest your head on the
cushions, like a young empress laying down her warrior's
helmet filled with roses, your symbolic flower.

M'introduire dans ton histoire
C'est en héros effarouché
S'il a du talon nu touché
Quelque gazon de territoire

A des glaciers attentatoire
Je ne sais le naïf péché
Que tu n'auras pas empêché
De rire très haut sa victoire

Dis si je ne suis pas joyeux
Tonnerre et rubis aux moyeux
De voir en l'air que ce feu troue

Avec des royaumes épars
Comme mourir pourpre la roue
Du seul vespéral de mes chars.

When I first entered your life I was an
ascetic frightened at the slightest contact
with earthly realities.
Anxious only to scale cold, intellectual
heights, I was unacquainted with the sins
of the flesh, which were soon to win,
however, a happy and joyful victory which
you did nothing to prevent.
How glad I now am to see in the sky the fiery
disc of the sun setting among scattered clouds,
like the wheel of a chariot with rubies fixed
to the hub and accompanied by the rumble of
thunder; for my nights are now given over to
pleasure and I seek no other source of light
after the sun has set.

O si chère de loin et proche et blanche, si
Délicieusement toi, Mary, que je songe
A quelque baume rare émané par mensonge
Sur aucun bouquetier de cristal obscurci

Le sais-tu, oui! Pour moi voici des ans, voici
Toujours que ton sourire éblouissant prolonge
La même rose avec son bel été qui plonge
Dans autrefois et puis dans le futur aussi.

Mon cœur qui dans les nuits parfois cherche à s'entendre
Ou de quel dernier mot t'appeler le plus tendre
S'exalte en celui rien que chuchoté de sœur

N'était, très grand trésor et tête si petite,
Que tu m'enseignes bien toute une autre douceur
Tout bas par le baiser seul dans tes cheveux dite.

Do you know that from both far and near your white skin
is so deliciously dear to me, Mary, that it reminds me of
some perfume so rare that it has never been given off by
any bouquet of flowers in an invisible crystal vase!
For years now, for ever, it seems to me, your dazzling smile
has continued to bloom like the same rose of summer rooted
deep in the past and in the future too.
My heart, which sometimes in the night tries to hear its own
beating, or to decide what would be the perfect term of utter
tenderness to apply to you, fixes on the gently whispered
word: "Sister"; were it not, my dearest love, that, with your
sweet face, you teach me a tenderness of quite another kind,
softly spoken into your hair by kisses alone.

Mes bouquins refermés sur le nom de Paphos,
Il m'amuse d'élire avec le seul génie
Une ruine, par mille écumes bénie
Sous l'hyacinthe au loin de ses jours triomphaux.

Coure le froid avec ses silences de faux,
Je n'y hululerai pas de vide nénie
Si ce très blanc ébat au ras du sol dénie
A tout site l'honneur du paysage faux.

Ma faim qui d'aucuns fruits ici ne se régale
Trouve en leur docte manque une saveur égale:
Qu'un éclate de chair humain et parfumant!

Le pied sur quelque guivre où notre amour tisonne,
Je pense plus longtemps peut-être éperdument
A l'autre, au sein brûlé d'une antique amazone.

Having closed the book I have been reading about Paphos
I am whiling away the time, with only my creative genius
to help me, by visualising, among the distant spring
hyacinths, its ruined temple of Venus beside the countless
waves, clad as it once was in the purple hangings of its
days of glory.
Even though the snow should begin to fall, silently
levelling everything, I shall not utter any vain
complaint if the white flakes, swirling along the ground,
obliterate the site on which I am trying to re-create my
imaginary landscape.
I no longer need any objects of this world to feed my
imagination and derive an equal intellectual pleasure
from dispensing with their presence. Even if the perfumed
shape of a woman's breast is revealed to my gaze, as I stand
by the hearth where our love is being rekindled, with my
foot resting on some carving in the form of a serpent, my
thoughts turn more and more, even perhaps completely, to
another, non-existent breast, whose destruction I seem to
see in the embers, of a legendary Amazon.

La chevelure vol d'une flamme à l'extrême
Occident de désirs pour la tout déployer
Se pose (je dirais mourir un diadème)
Vers le front couronné son ancien foyer

Mais sans or soupirer que cette vive nue
L'ignition du feu toujours intérieur
Originellement la seule continue
Dans le joyau de l'œil véridique ou rieur

Une nudité de héros tendre diffame
Celle qui ne mouvant astre ni feux au doigt
Rien qu'à simplifier avec gloire la femme
Accomplit par son chef fulgurante l'exploit

De semer de rubis le doute qu'elle écorche
Ainsi qu'une joyeuse et tutélaire torche.

Her hair was once like a leaping flame, but now, as
the desire to loose these tresses finally wanes, they
symbolically coil themselves, like a fading diadem,
round her head to form a crown set upon the source
from which the flame once sprang.
But there is no need now to long for the vivid cloud
of her hair since the light of the inner fire of love,
of which her hair was once the only sign, continues
to shine in the sparkle of her frank and laughing eyes.
A lover's naked body would be an insult to someone
who, although her fingers, with their rings and jewels,
no longer loosen her hair, is still the glorious essence of
womanhood, with a radiance that enables her face alone to
accomplish the feat of replacing with a feeling of immense
good fortune all my doubts and fears which are as if burned
away in the flame of a joyful and protective torch.

Dame
     sans trop d'ardeur à la fois enflammant
La rose qui cruelle ou déchiré et lasse
Même du blanc habit de pourpre le délace
Pour ouïr dans sa chair pleurer le diamant

Oui sans ces crises de rosée et gentiment
Ni brise quoique, avec, le ciel orageux passe
Jalouse d'apporter je ne sais quel espace
Au simple jour le jour très vrai du sentiment,

Ne te semble-t-il pas, disons, que chaque année
Dont sur ton front renaît la grâce spontanée
Suffise selon quelque apparence et pour moi

Comme un éventail frais dans la chambre s'étonne
A raviver du peu qu'il faut ici d'émoi
Toute notre native amitié monotone.

Lady, without excess of passion kindling desire in the rosy
flesh which, whether active or passive, tired of its red
sheath remaining empty, opens to feel within it the precious
tears; without these moments of passion, although the days
of ardour are also past and you are now in gentler mood,
wanting to bring a sense of freshness into the sincere and
frank relationship between us, does it not seem to you,
do you not agree with me that every passing year brings
a fresh, new graciousness to your face and that, for me,
this is clearly enough to renew, with what little touch of
emotion we now need, like a waving fan refreshing a room,
all our long and placid friendship.

ELEGIES II
1885 – 1898

HOMMAGE

Le silence déjâ funèbre d'une moire
Dispose plus qu'un pli seul sur le mobilier
Que doit un tassement du principal pilier
Précipiter avec le manque de mémoire.

Notre si vieil ébat triomphal du grimoire,
Hiéroglyphes dont s'exalte le millier
A propager de l'aile un frisson familier!
Enfouissez-le moi plutôt dans une armoire.

Du souriant fracas originel haï
Entre elles de clartés maîtresses a jailli
Jusque vers un parvis né pour leur simulacre,

Trompettes tout haut d'or pâmé sur les vélins,
Le dieu Richard Wagner irradiant un sacre
Mal tu par l'encre même en sanglots sibyllins.

HOMAGE TO WAGNER

The funereal silence of a shroud is already beginning to
spread its folds across the contents of my mind which
will finally be consigned to oblivion when I myself, the
supporting pillar of the temple sheltering these ideas,
am shortly lowered into the earth.
How long ago it was that we triumphantly talked of
secret ciphers, hieroglyphics rising up in their thousands
to provoke the old familiar reaction! All this should now
be stuffed into the back of some drawer; for it is Richard
Wagner who, from the captivating and at first hated
clamour of strident golden trumpets noted down on the score
with compelling silences between, has soared up like a god
to attain the heights of the temple at Bayreuth created for
the performance of his operas, radiant with a glory that not
even the esoteric nature of musical notation can obscure.

SALUT

Rien, cette écume, vierge vers
A ne désigner que la coupe;
Telle loin se noie une troupe
De sirènes mainte à l'envers.

Nous naviguons, ô mes divers
Amis, moi déjà sur la poupe
Vous l'avant fastueux qui coupe
Le flot de foudres et d'hivers.

Une ivresse belle m'engage
Sans craindre même son tangage
De porter debout ce salut

Solitude, récif, étoile
A n'importe ce qui valut
Le blanc souci de notre toile.

TOAST

These simple lines have no other importance than their
rhythm; just as the bubbling surface of my untouched
glass of champagne serves no other purpose than to
indicate the shape of the cup; both are like a band of
seductive sirens tumbling over in the distant waves.
We, around this table, are sailing on a ship, my friends,
and I stand here on the poop, while you form the splendid
prow, cutting through the stormy, wintry waves.
The strong spirit within me urges me not to worry about
the rocking of the boat but to stand up boldly and give
this toast, whether the outcome of our voyage be the
solitude of an uncompleted task, the shipwreck of failure
or the haven of success, to whatever goal has inspired
the steadfast purpose that has driven our white sails.

A la nue accablante tu
Basse de basalte et de laves
A même les échos esclaves
Par une trompe sans vertu

Quel sépulcral naufrage (tu
Le sais, écume, mais y baves)
Suprême une entre les épaves
Abolit le mât dévêtu

Ou cela que furibond faute
De quelque perdition haute
Tout l'abîme vain éployé

Dans le si blanc cheveu qui traîne
Avarement aura noyé
Le flanc enfant d'une sirène

Unannounced to the heavy, lowering clouds,
as grey as basalt or lava, by a silent bugle
which fails to awaken its usual echoes, what
tragic shipwreck, known only to the heedless
waves, of a supremely splendid vessel has
swallowed up the mast stripped of its sails?
Or is it rather that, furious at not having
a worthy victim, the sea will prove to have
expended its rage in vain and to have spite-
fully drowned, in the white line of foam like
a strand of trailing hair, a siren not yet
fully grown.

LE TOMBEAU DE CHARLES BAUDELAIRE

Le temple enseveli divulgue par la bouche
Sépulcral d'égout bavant boue et rubis
Abominablement quelque idole Anubis
Tout le museau flambé comme un aboi farouche

Ou que le gaz récent torde la mèche louche
Essuyeuse on le sait des opprobres subis
Il allume hagard un immortel pubis
Dont le vol selon le réverbère découche

Quel feuillage séché dans les cités sans soir
Votif pourra bénir comme elle se rasseoir
Contre le marbre vainement de Baudelaire

Au voile qui la ceint absente avec frissons
Celle son Ombre même un poison tutélaire
Toujours à respirer si nous en périssons.

ELEGY TO CHARLES BAUDELAIRE

Baudelaire's poetry is like a buried temple revealing, through
the sepulchral mouth of a sewer spewing mud and rubies, some
repulsive, Anubis-like idol, its blackened muzzle opened in a
savage snarl.
Or it is like the recently introduced gas jets when they twist
their dim flame (intended, as we know, to put an end to the
scandalous scenes in the streets of Paris) so that its light falls
on the shameless hip of some woman practising the age-old
profession who moves in and out of the circle of light cast by
the flickering street-lamp.
What withered laurel leaves in the land of eternal day would
better serve as the symbol of the poet's divine genius than
such a woman, sitting waiting in vain beside Baudelaire's
marble tomb, for, as the trembling circle of light passes
to and fro across her, she seems like his very ghost, the
personification of his poetry, whose poisonous yet salutary
effect it is our duty to experience, however painful it may be.

TOMBEAU DE VERLAINE

Le noir roc courroucé que la bise le roule
Ne s'arrêtera ni sous de pieuses mains
Tâtant sa ressemblance avec les maux humains
Comme pour en bénir quelque funeste moule.

Ici presque toujours si le ramier roucoule
Cet immatériel deuil opprime de maints
Nubiles plis l'astre mûri des lendemains
Dont un scintillement argentera la foule.

Qui cherche, parcourant le solitaire bond
Tantôt extérieur de notre vagabond –
Verlaine? Il est caché parmi l'herbe, Verlaine

A ne surprendre que naïvement d'accord
La lèvre sans y boire ou tarir son haleine
Un peu profond ruisseau calomnié la mort.

ELEGY TO VERLAINE

The dark stone of Verlaine's tomb, as the wind swirls round it,
recalls the querulous nature of the man himself, who would
have been angry if the wind had pushed him along and yet
would have been equally unwilling to halt among those pious
creatures counting all the ills his flesh was heir to, as if devoutly
thankful to see in him an awful example.
Here in the cemetery the cooing of the doves forms a kind of
veil of mourning whose folds blur as yet the bright star into
which Verlaine will grow in future years and whose brilliance
will shed its light throughout the world.
Those who pursued Verlaine during his lonely, restless,
vagabond life which has now ended, must look for him among
the grass where he is hidden and where, with simple acceptance,
but without its waters passing his lips or stilling his voice as a
poet, he has come across the Styx, a mere shallow stream that it
is wrong to insult with the name of death.

Au seul souci de voyager
Outre une Inde splendide et trouble
– Ce salut soit le messager
Du temps, cap que ta poupe double

Comme sur quelque vergue bas
Plongeante avec la caravelle
Ecumait toujours en ébats
Un oiseau d'annonce nouvelle

Qui criait monotonement
Sans que la barre ne varie
Un inutile gisement
Nuit, désespoir et pierrerie

Par son chant reflété jusqu'au
Sourire du pâle Vasco.

To life's sole goal of sailing onwards,
beyond the troubled splendour of India,
I give this salute as a messenger from
the shores of time, whose cape of four
hundred years your ship is rounding;
just as, on the yard-arm, plunging deep
into the waves, of your caravel, a foam-
flecked bird once fluttered, the bearer
of fresh tidings.
It ceaselessly repeated, without the tiller
ever shifting from its position, that the
vessel was pursuing a useless course towards
darkness and despair, relieved only by the
light of an occasional star, the message of
its song being reflected in the smile of
resignation and resolution on the pale face
of Vasco da Gama.

FINAL CONSOLATION
1897

UN COUP DE DÉS JAMAIS N'ABOLIRA LE HASARD

NOTE

As indicated in the introduction (pp. 12–13) the way in which the words of *Un coup de dés* are set out in the 'frame' of the double page has an important pictorial effect. Consequently the English translation cannot be put on facing pages. It has therefore been interleaved with the French text, despite the difficulty that this entails in reading the two in parallel. An attempt has also been made to follow the pattern of the French text in the English text although it cannot of course be precisely reproduced in translation. Page numbers and page headings have been omitted so as not to distract from the pictorial effect.

UN COUP DE DÉS

A CAST OF THE DICE

JAMAIS

QUAND BIEN MÊME LANCÉ DANS DES CIRCONSTANCES

ÉTERNELLES

DU FOND D'UN NAUFRAGE

WILL NEVER

EVEN WHEN MADE

IN DESPERATE CIRCUMSTANCES

FROM THE DEPTHS OF A SHIPWRECK

SOIT
        que

                l'Abîme

        blanchi
                étale
                    furieux
                            sous une inclinaison
                                plane désespérément

                                        d'aile

                                    la sienne
                                            par

avance retombée d'un mal à dresser le vol
et couvrant les jaillissements
coupant au ras les bonds

très à l'intérieur résume

l'ombre enfouie dans la profondeur par cette voile alternative

jusqu'adapter
à l'envergure

sa béante profondeur en tant que la coque

d'un bâtiment

penché de l'un ou l'autre bord

SUCH
    that

        the unfathomable ocean –

white
    at full tide
      raging

          beneath the despairing sweep
           of the lowering sky

               joined to it

             like a fallen wing

that has succumbed too soon to its inability to soar aloft
                                     covering the flung spray
                              cutting into the leaping waves –

          offers to one's inner vision

      the alternative interpretation of a sail casting its shadow
      over the depths; so that

                           attached to
                                this spreading sail

                  a gaping trough between two waves

                    resembles the hull of a ship

                  listing to one side or the other

LE MAITRE

surgi
    inférant

           de cette conflagration

                que se

             comme on menace

         l'unique Nombre qui ne peut pas

                    hésite
             cadavre par le bras
plutôt
    que de jouer
       en maniaque chenu
          la partie
       au nom des flots
                  un

            naufrage cela

hors d'anciens calculs
où la manoeuvre avec l'âge oubliée

jadis il empoignait la barre

à ses pieds
de l'horizon unanime

prépare
s'agite et mêle
au poing qui l'étreindrait
un destin et les vents

être un autre

Esprit
pour le jeter
dans la tempête
en reployer la division et passer fier

écarté du secret qu'il détient

envahit le chef
coule en barbe soumise

direct de l'homme

sans nef
n'importe
où vaine

THE MASTER

having floated to the surface
and inferring

from the glowing sunset

that

which seems to be defying

the one Number that is to be

hesitates
although already virtually a corpse
holding out at arm's
to throw the dice
like a white-haired madman
on behalf of the waves
one of which

swamping

incapable now of the former reckoning
(his skills forgotten with advancing years)

by which he once guided the tiller

on the endless horizon
    beyond his feet
    as he lies on the water

the dice are preparing
    forming and creating
        gripped within his clenched fist
destiny and the storm

his alone

        (his spirit urges him
            to fling the dice
                into the tempest
      to reshape the number and pass proudly on)

length the secret he possesses

sweeps over his head
runs down his face like a flowing beard

the man himself directly

    without his ship
           lost
              and useless

ancestralement à n'ouvrir pas la main
crispée
par delà l'inutile tête

legs en la disparition

à quelqu'un
ambigu

l'ultérieur démon immémorial

ayant
de contrées nulles
induit
le vieillard vers cette conjonction suprême avec la probabilité

celui
son ombre puérile
caressée et polie et rendue et lavée
assouplie par la vague et soustraite
aux durs os perdus entre les ais

né
d'un ébat
la mer par l'aïeul tentant ou l'aïeul contre la mer
une chance oiseuse

Fiançailles

dont
le voile d'illusion rejailli leur hantise
ainsi que le fantôme d'un geste

chancellera
s'affalera

folie

N'ABOLIRA

(he hesitates)
endlessly failing to open his hand
                    tightly closed
                above his dying head

        his legacy disappearing with him
        instead of being bequeathed

                not to one definite person

            but to the eternal and infinite human spirit

which has spurred the old man on
                    to leave the quiet shores
for this supreme encounter with probable defeat

                    that spirit
                        which is like a child
that has been cradled and fondled before being returned washed
                and smoothed by the waves and freed
        from the hard bones lost among the timbers of the sunken vessel

                a spirit born
                        of a clash between
the old man and the sea the latter vainly trying through the
former or the former vainly struggling against the latter
                to throw the dice

                                    An alliance
whose vague illusions will one day be dispelled and its obsession
along with its ghostly gesture

                    will falter
                    and collapse

                        revealed as folly

ABOLISH

COMME SI

Une insinuation

au silence

dans quelque proche

voltige

simple

enroulée avec ironie
                 ou
                      le mystère
                                   précipité
                                           hurlé

tourbillon d'hilarité et d'horreur

autour du gouffre
                         sans le joncher
                                   ni fuir

                   et en berce le vierge indice

                                           COMME SI

AS IF

A discreet roll

which would be received

which would promptly raise

these two solutions hover

of the dice

with an ironic silence
              or
                    a sudden
                            ostentatious
                            revelation of one's secret
a storm of laughter and horror

above the waves
      without ever being definitely settled upon
                    or definitely discarded

          in the fond hope of some sign that never occurs

                                                  AS IF

plume solitaire éperdue

sauf

que la rencontre ou l'effleure une toque de minuit
et immobilise
au velours chiffonné par un esclaffement sombre

cette blancheur rigide

dérisoire
en opposition au ciel
trop
pour ne pas marquer
exigüment
quiconque

prince amer de l'écueil

s'en coiffe comme de l'héroïque
irrésistible mais contenu
par sa petite raison virile

en foudre

lost and lonely quill

were it not

that the cap of the midnight sky lies against it or near it
and fixes
into the velvet creased as if by a grim burst of laughter

its whiteness stiff

and derisory

contrasting with the sky

too sharply

not to emphasise

the tiny stature

of whoever

a bitter shipwrecked prince

wears the feathered cap as he does the heroic
captivating (though restrained by the limited
scope of his mind however vigorous it may be

and powerful)

soucieux

       expiatoire et pubère

                muet

          La lucide et seigneurial aigrette

              au front invisible

       scintille

          puis ombrage

   une stature mignonne ténébreuse

     en sa torsion de sirène

    par d'impatientes squames ultimes

rire

que

SI

de vertige

debout

   le temps
       de souffleter
bifurquées

     un roc

   faux manoir
       tout de suite
          évaporé en brumes

       qui imposa
         une borne à l'infini

anxious

    apologetic and hesitant

            quiet

The pale and haughty feather
the invisible forehead
shimmers for a moment
then casts its shadow over
the vague seductive form of
a lissom siren who appears

impatiently her scaly

            smile

                    which

                        IF

floats above

for long enough
                to slap
fish's tail against

            a rock

a deceptive resting place
            which promptly
                vanished into thin air

                    but which formed a barrier
                    to further exploration
                        of the ideal world

C'ÉTAIT
issu stellaire

CE SERAIT

pire

non

davantage ni moins

indifféremment mais autant

LE NOMBRE

EXISTÂT-IL
autrement qu'hallucination éparse d'agonie

COMMENÇÂT-IL ET CESSÂT-IL
sourdant que nié et clos quand apparu
enfin
par quelque profusion répandu en rareté
SE CHIFFRÂT-IL

évidence de la somme pour peu qu'une
ILLUMINÂT-IL

LE HASARD

Choit
la plume
rythmique suspens du sinistre

s'ensevelir
aux écumes originelles
naguères d'où sursauta son délire jusqu'à une cime
flétrie
par la neutralité identique du gouffre

IF IT WAS

like something foretold in the stars

IT WOULD STILL BE

not worse

nor more

nor less than

but the same as

ONE'S OWN DESTINY

CAN IT REALLY HAVE EXISTED

other than as the vague illusion of a dying man

CAN IT REALLY HAVE HAD
A BEGINNING AND AN END

trickling out secretly and cautiously at first
and finally
with a certain profusion among the few

DID IT REALLY FORM AN AMOUNT

substantial enough to bear witness to the total
that might have been reached

CAN IT REALLY HAVE SHED LIGHT

CHANCE

The pen

falls

that has swung to and fro
postponing the disaster

and plunges deep
into the sea from which it originally sprang
and from which its ambition leapt to a height
hated
by the bland uniformity of those left behind

RIEN

de la mémorable crise
ou se fût
l'événement

accompli en vue de tout résultat nul

humain

N'AURA EU LIEU
une élévation ordinaire verse l'absence

QUE LE LIEU
inférieur clapotis quelconque comme pour disperser l'acte vide
abruptement qui sinon
par son mensonge
eût fondé
la perdition

dans ces parages

du vague

en quoi toute réalité se dissout

NOTHING

of this memorable crisis
otherwise the deed
might have been

accomplished with a view to achieving
a superhuman goal

WILL HAVE TAKEN PLACE
for a level gaze reveals nothing

ONLY THE PLACE ITSELF REMAINS
with the vague murmur of the waves seeming to want to efface
as quickly as possible the abortive attempt
which otherwise might have created
a myth about
the disappearance

in these waters
of the ideal
into which all reality dissolves

EXCEPTÉ

    à l'altitude

        PEUT-ÊTRE

            aussi loin qu'un endroit

fusionne avec au-delà

hors l'intérêt
quant à lui signalé
en général
selon telle obliquité par telle déclivité
de feux

vers
ce doit être
le Septentrion aussi Nord

UNE CONSTELLATION

froide d'oubli et de désuétude
pas tant
qu'elle n'énumère
sur quelque surface vacante et supérieure
le heurt successif
sidéralement
d'un compte total en formation

veillant
doutant
roulant
brillant et méditant

avant de s'arrêter
à quelque point dernier qui le sacre

Toute Pensée émet un Coup de Dés

EXCEPT THAT
      high above
            PERHAPS
                  far away where a point on earth

is prolonged into the beyond

                    outside any interest
                    accorded to it
                              in a general way
with regard to the oblique angle or slanting line
                              of its stars

        towards
              what must be
                    the Northern sky shines

                         A CONSTELLATION

              cold with neglect and disuse
                    but not so much so
                    that it cannot count
              on some empty space high in the sky
              the appearance one after the other
                                   of stars
              as they make up a final total

watching
        wondering
                    rolling through the heavens
                         shining and pondering

                    before finally halting
              when the destined number is at last attained

              Every Thought means a Cast of the Dice

NOTES

p. 18
The paradoxical sadness of this love poem could be no more than traditional romantic melancholy, but it could also be the consequence of Mallarmé perceiving in his future wife, Maria Gerhard, the reincarnation of his mother who had died when he was five years old and who is no doubt the figure appearing in the last few lines as he remembers her from his childhood dreams. Even at this early stage Mallarmé seems therefore to be irresistibly drawn to the world beyond reality.

p. 20
'Les Fenêtres' was written in May 1863 and the metaphor of the dying man may well have been inspired by the death of Mallarmé's father the previous month. The curiously dismissive reference in the third verse to the first taste of love being long past may reflect the problems that occurred in Mallarmé's relationship with Maria Gerhard before they finally married in August 1863.

p. 22
In the ninth verse of 'Les Fenêtres' it seems certain that 'Bêtise' cannot have its usual meaning of 'stupidity' and must have its etymological meaning of 'animality', thus echoing the reference in the sixth verse to men 'wallowing' and to women 'suckling their offspring'.

p. 32
'Le Pitre châtié' is the first of Mallarmé's really 'difficult' texts. The word 'pitre' means both 'clown' and 'turncoat'. Both senses are present in the poem, the clown or actor sense in the imagery and the turncoat or traitor sense in the meaning. A further difficulty arises from the complex analogy running through the poem between actor and author. Thus in line 3 'plume' is both 'feather' and 'pen', 'quinquets' is both 'foot-lights' and 'reading lamp', the word 'toile' in line 4 refers not only to the fabric of the theatre curtain but, in the sense of a painter's canvas, refers also, by extension, to the poet's writing paper, 'peau' in line 12 refers metaphorically to the actor's costume and also to the rôle assumed by the poet, while the word 'fard' in the same line refers to the actor's make-up and to the alternative identity sought by the poet. It should be noted

that line 12 is to be read as an exclamation in parenthesis: 'How dark and offensive seemed the costume I had donned', although the exclamation is in fact addressed directly to the costume: 'How dark and offensive you seemed, costume, when you clothed me'

p. 36

Although no one would dispute that the figure of the swan in this celebrated sonnet represents the poet, or, strictly speaking, a day in the life of the poet, by no means all critics would agree that there are two swans, and therefore two days, in the poem, a 'cygne d'autrefois' symbolising Mallarmé as he once was and a 'cygne d'aujourd'hui' symbolising him as he now is. Those who think that there is only one swan see it, in the final lines, as covering itself with scorn and see its 'useless exile' as a reference to its enforced inactivity. The alternative interpretation adopted here sees the 'cygne d'aujourd'hui', now firmly deter-mined not to seek refuge in facile verse, as pouring scorn on the 'cygne d'autrefois' for having done so. The image of a bird symbolising a day may spring from the rays of the rising sun looking like the feathers of a wing (see 'Sainte' p. 64). More specifically Mallarmé may be playing on the words 'cygne' and 'signe', since the day's work for the poet consists of making signs on paper. The analogy between a sheet of paper and a sheet of ice is a more obvious one, from which it follows that the 'transparent glacier des vols qui n'ont pas fui' is the block of blank sheets of paper representing a succession of days when Mallarmé has failed to write anything on 'le vide papier que la blancheur défend', as he was shortly to put it in 'Brise marine' (see p. 60).

p. 66

The word 'console' in the last line of the first sonnet of this trilogy probably refers to the kind of two-legged table propped against a wall that can be used for shielding a fireplace, but it may refer to the carved supporting columns of a mantelpiece.

p. 68

As so often Mallarmé is using a word in two senses in line 13 of this sonnet where the word 'expirer' means both 'to breathe out' and 'to expire', as it also does in line 13 of 'Quelle soie aux baumes de temps' (see p. 94).

p. 72

The word 'ptyx' in line 5 of this 'sonnet en -ix', as it is sometimes called, does not exist in French and a wide variety of interpretations have been suggested – quite needlessly since Mallarmé himself helpfully defines it in the next line as a 'bibelot d'inanité sonore'. There is only one object which frequently serves as a decorative trinket and which, although empty, is full of sound – a sea shell. Mallarmé doubly emphasises this point in line 8 when he further describes the 'ptyx' as being the only object by which emptiness is honoured and uses an expression which can be understood phonetically as 'le Néant sonore' – 'the sonorous emptiness'. Two final points are that a sea shell often functions as an ash-tray – as it does here in lines 4 and 5 – and can equally be used to scoop up water, as it does in line 7.

p. 74

It is typical of Mallarmé's ingenuity and ambiguity that the last line could also be read, phonetically, as 'Que c'est un astre en fête allumé le génie' – that genius is a shining, festive star – although this adjectival version is more generalised and more static than the verbal version he uses which emphasises that the coming of a specific genius (namely himself) has been marked by a festive star lighting up the sky.

p. 78

In line 5 of 'Toast funèbre' the expression 'l'on ignore mal' is a negative variant of the common formula 'on sait bien'.

p. 84

The significance of the date is that 2 November is All Souls' Day. The sonnet is addressed to a grieving husband by his dead wife, a friend of Mallarmé's, who had died four years before in 1873. The tercets are especially noteworthy for the softening effect of the accumulation of 'f','v', 'm' and 's' sounds and for the gently insistent murmur of the final line, admirably matching sound with sense. Perhaps because of its very personal note Mallarmé did not include this poem in his edition of his *Poésies*.

p. 90

Verses 10, 11 and 12 of 'Prose' form a particularly long and complex sentence, even by Mallarmé's standards, which has meant bringing forward in the translation the last line of verse 12. Most commentators assume that the 'enfant' and the 'elle' of verse 13 are one and the same, but in an earlier version of the poem the word 'enfant' does not exist and the antecedent of the word 'elle' is the 'sœur sensée et tendre' of verse 9. The general sense of the poem also suggests that 'enfant' refers to the poet and 'elle' to the elder sister figure of his muse. Her command: 'Anastase!' (from the Greek 'anastasis') means: 'Rise up!' and as the opening word of the poem: 'Hyperbole!', also means, etymologically, a leap upwards, the argument has come full circle, with the initial question: 'Can I rise triumphantly to my task?' being finally answered – or at least the poet's muse urges him to answer it. Most commentators also assume that since the 'glaïeul' (gladiolus) in the last line of the poem belongs to the iris family it must therefore be one of the ideal flowers referred to in earlier verses. But again the logic of the argument suggests that, on the contrary, it is a mortal flower which will overwhelm the 'beau idéal' the poet is seeking ('Pulchérie' is from the Latin for 'beauty') unless he hastens to complete his task. It is worth adding that whereas the word 'iris', with its connotations of a goddess and a rainbow, has intimations of immortality, 'gladiolus', which is the Latin for a sword, has contrary intimations of mortality.

p. 94

There has been much discussion about the flags in line 5. It has been suggested that they are celebrating the 14 July 1884, but the fact that Mallarmé is sacrificing 'la gloire' to 'l'amour' suggests that they are more likely to be those which were flown on 2 October 1884 to celebrate the bicentenary of the death of Pierre Corneille whose heroes are renowned for having, on the contrary, sacrificed 'l'amour' to 'la gloire'.

p. 96

The fact that this poem too is on the theme of 'la gloire' being abandoned in favour of 'l'amour' lends support to the suggestion that 'Quelle soie...' refers to the bicentenary of the death of Pierre Corneille.

p. 98

'M'introduire dans ton histoire' is the first of four of Mallarmé's last poems, along with 'La chevelure...', 'A la nue...' and 'Le Tombeau de Baudelaire', in which he abandons punctuation, except for the use of two brackets enclosing a parenthesis in line 3 of 'La chevelure...' and two similar punctuation marks enclosing a further parenthesis indicated by two commas in the second verse of 'A la nue...'. It may be that he found punctuation inadequate to cope with his convoluted syntax and consequently felt that he might as well dispense with it altogether.

p. 100

The accumulation of negatives in lines 3 and 4 of 'O si chère de loin...' may be light-hearted in tone but it is characteristic of Mallarmé and is yet another way of evoking 'l'absente de tous bouquets' (see Introduction pp. 8 and 9). The very last word of the poem is an intriguing example of Mallarmé's extraordinary ability to match sound and sense, in that the final mute 'e' preceded by 't' imitates the sound of the kiss on which the sonnet ends. He nevertheless excluded it from his edition of his *Poésies*.

p. 102

Mallarmé chose 'Mes bouquins refermés...' as the closing poem of his edition of his *Poésies*, perhaps simply because of the aptness of those first words but also perhaps, more subtly, because lines 9 and 10 admirably and succinctly express in yet another memorable phrase Mallarmé's obsession with the intellectual pursuit of the immaterial world. The lines are impossible to translate satisfactorily because of the multiple senses of the word 'fruit' which provides the transition from the real landscape, which he no longer needs as the basis on which to construct his imaginary temple, to the fruit-shaped breast of Méry Laurent on which his gaze falls in line 11 and to which he prefers the imaginary breast of the Amazon. It should be noted that the exclamation mark at the end of line 11 does not indicate a break in syntax, so the appeal for the naked perfumed breast to burst upon his sight (rather than to burst in any actual physical sense – a gruesome and unlikely interpretation) is to be read in the sense of 'Even if...'. In line 4 it seems likely that 'hyacinthe' too has a double sense, referring both to the flowers Mallarmé sees in his garden, as he tries to visualise there the temple of Venus at Paphos, and the purple colour of the hangings in which the temple was a clad in its days of glory.

p. 104

Line 5 of 'La chevelure...' is the subject of much disagreement – is 'or' the noun meaning 'gold' and 'que' the conjunction 'that'? Or is 'or' the adverb 'now' and does 'que' along with 'sans' have the meaning of 'only'? Does the line therefore mean: 'Its golden colour having faded, I want the vivid cloud of her hair…to continue etc.'; or, as proposed here, does it mean: 'Without now longing for the vivid cloud of her hair, her inner radiance continues etc.'. This difference in interpretation does not, however, substantially affect the sense of the poem. It is to be noted that in line 12 the word 'fulgurante' is feminine and so does not agree with 'chef'. It is now therefore Méry as a person who possesses a kind of radiance, not solely her hair. It should also be noted that her once sensually cascading tresses are now more primly coiled round her head so that it is her 'chef' rather than her 'chevelure' which now has its effect upon Mallarmé. Technically the poem is an astonishing 'tour de force' in that, so as to re-create in the mind of the reader the flame-like quality of Méry Laurent's flowing red hair, it begins with 'chevelure' and ends with 'torche' and in between these two poles Mallarmé manages to insert in almost every one of the fourteen lines of the sonnet a word, or words, evocative of light and radiance – 'flamme', 'occident', 'diadème', 'couronné', 'foyer', 'or', 'ignition', 'feu', 'joyau', 'astre', 'feux', 'fulgurante', 'rubis', and 'écorche'. 'Ecorcher' actually means 'to flay' or 'to skin', but the context clearly suggests that here Mallarmé is giving the word the sense of 'to burn', as in its English etymological counterpart. He had in fact noted the relationship between the two words in his *Les Mots anglais*.

p. 106

A first version of this sonnet began with the name 'Méry', later changed to the less specific 'Dame'. The chief bone of contention in the poem is the meaning of the word 'blanc' in line 3, but since nothing can, at one and the same time, be both white and purple, it seems logical to conclude that 'blanc' must have here its alternative meaning of 'empty'. If the opening quatrain does have the specific sexual sense attributed to it here it could explain why Mallarmé excluded this sonnet from his edition of his *Poésies*.

p. 110

The interpretation of the first quatrain of 'Hommage à Wagner' proposed by some critics who saw it as referring to the collapse of the theatre in late 19th century France was disproved by the publication in 1983 of a letter by Mallarmé making it clear that it is concerned with the collapse of poetry. Whether it is poetry in general or his own poetry in particular is a matter of dispute, but the latter interpretation is adopted here in view of the fact that line 5 is surely an ironic allusion to the former optimism of 'Prose pour des Esseintes' whose opening lines contain the words 'triomphalement' and 'grimoire'. Similarly line 6 mockingly recalls Mallarmé's exaltation in verses 8 and 9 of 'Prose' as innumerable ideal forms rose up before his eyes. In disenchantedly describing his attempts to give a new dimension to poetry as 'un frisson familier' in line 7 Mallarmé may well be playing on Hugo's celebrated comment to Baudelaire: 'Vous créez un frisson nouveau'. Line 8 is reminiscent of Alceste's scathing comment on Oronte's sonnet in Molière's *Le Misanthrope*: 'Franchement, il est bon à mettre au cabinet'.

p. 112

Mallarmé chose 'Salut' as the introductory poem in his edition of his *Poésies*, perhaps as a disappointed comment on the worth of this volume of 'études en vue de mieux' as he called them and as he saw them. As befits a poem recited at a literary banquet it is a light-hearted piece with complex puns on 'vers' and 'verre' and on 'coupe' as 'cup' and as the 'cut' or 'shape' of a poem. There is also the extended analogy between the dining table and a ship, the use of 'ivresse' in both an alcoholic and a literary sense and of 'tangage' referring both to the metaphorical ship rolling in the waves and to Mallarmé being unsteady on his feet, and, no doubt, to the buffeting his poems were receiving at the hands of hostile critics. Finally 'toile' is the cloth on the dining table, the canvas of the sail of the ship and, via the canvas of a painter, the paper on which the poet writes.

p. 114

The word 'tu' at the end of line 1 of 'A la nue...' is the past participle of 'taire' meaning 'to silence'; so the sepulchral shipwreck of line 5 has been silenced, or unannounced, to the clouds, by a bugle lacking in strength or power – an old meaning of 'vertu'. In line 9 'cela' is taken here to be the demonstrative pronoun, so 'ou cela que' is tantamount to 'ou est-ce que'. Some critics, however, suggest that 'cela' is the past tense of the verb 'celer' meaning 'to conceal', in which case the translation would be 'or did the shipwreck conceal the fact that...'. This would make little or no difference to the general sense of the sonnet which, as indicated in the introduction, p. 12, expresses Mallarmé's fear that his death will mean the loss, not of a great poet, but of a mere versifier who has yielded to the temptation to waste his time on minor writings.

p. 120

Most commentators agree that 'gisement' in line 11 of 'Au seul souci de voyager' is meant in its maritime sense of a ship's bearing or direction rather than in its mining sense of a stratum of rock and that consequently the word 'pierrerie' in the following line is used metaphorically in the sense of a star, with the three nouns in line 12 being reminiscent of and parallel to the 'solitude, récif, étoile' in line 12 of 'Salut'. But, as so often, both senses may well be intended, with the bird warning Vasco da Gama that he will find no more than the occasional precious stone to lighten the darkness and despondency of his explorations – as Mallarmé himself has done.

p. 123

For the layout of *Un coup de dés* the edition published by Mitsou Ronat, Change errant d'atelier, Paris, 1980 has been followed since it coincides with the proof copy, corrected by Mallarmé himself, of an edition by Lahure which was never actually published. A photograph of this corrected proof is reproduced in R.G. Cohn, *Mallarmé's Masterwork, New Findings*, Mouton & Co., The Hague, Paris, 1966. There are variations, mostly of a minor nature, between the placing of the words on the page in this definitive proof and in the editions currently available.

p. 125

In choosing the title and the theme of *Un coup de dés* did Mallarmé have in mind the two lines of the next to last scene of Shakespeare's *Richard III:*

I have set my life upon a cast
And I will stand the hazard of the die?

p. 136

In this marine context 'maître' refers to the master of the ship, but the word has, of course, a much wider meaning. In particular it is to be noted that Mallarmé uses it with reference to the poet Théophile Gautier in 'Toast Funèbre' and to himself in 'Ses purs ongles...'. This is the first of several indications that *Un coup de dés* is really concerned with the act of writing, or rather of publication. The black on white of the dice image and the presence of the writer's pen behind the feather image are other examples. It must be said, however, that few, if any, other critics would be quite so specific in interpreting the symbolism of *Un coup de dés*.

p. 150

Since 'plume' in French means both 'pen' and 'feather', 'quill' seems the best translation here. The verb 'voltiger' on the previous page marks the transition from the dice image to the feather/pen image, both of them symbolising the poet's uncertainty about setting things down in black and white.

pp. 152–53

Does the siren in her 'faux manoir... qui imposa une borne à l'infini' represent Méry Laurent (see Introduction p. 11)? Or docs she represent, less specifically, all the distractions of the material world which, in the late 1880s and 1890s, drew Mallarmé's attention away from the ideal world? Probably the latter, given the use of the term in the two sonnets written shortly before, 'Rien, cette écume, vierge vers' and 'A la nue accablante tu'.

p. 159

At this stage the 'pen' sense of the word 'plume' takes precedence over the 'feather' sense.

p. 165

It is interesting and no doubt significant that the concluding lines of *Un coup de dés* are set out not only in the shape of two dice which have finally been thrown and have fallen to reveal three and four dots respectively, but also in the shape of the constellation of the Great Bear with its slanting line of three stars and its rectangle of four stars. Mallarmé thus gives visual form to the quiet conviction he expresses in these lines that, however modest his achievements may appear, they will ultimately suffice to ensure the fulfilment of his destiny and the realisation of his ambition, proclaimed thirty years before in *Ses purs ongles,* to escape the confines of the real world and enter the ideal world beyond.